LIVE LONG AND . . .

LIVE LONG AND . . .

WHAT I LEARNED ALONG THE WAY

WILLIAM SHATNER
WITH DAVID FISHER

THORNDIKE PRESS

A part of Gale, a Cengage Company

Farmington Hills, Mich • San Francisco • New York • Waterville, Maine
Meriden, Conn • Mason, Ohio • Chicago

LIBRARY OF CONGRESS CIP DATA ON FILE.
CATALOGUING IN PUBLICATION FOR THIS BOOK
IS AVAILABLE FROM THE LIBRARY OF CONGRESS

ISBN-13: 978-1-4328-5955-8 (hardcover)

Published in 2018 by arrangement with Macmillan Publishing, LLC/St. Martin's Press

Printed in Mexico
1 2 3 4 5 6 7 22 21 20 19 18

I would like to dedicate this book to an old, old friend who is no longer with us. Carmen La Via was a young agent in Los Angeles when I arrived on the scene. We went through many manifestations of client/agent/friend. He moved to New York and he became my literary agent. We did a lot of work together, much of it really good. To show you how tough he was, at one point he had a "Do Not Resuscitate" sign posted on his door. He was given last rites and was given up for dead. But that tough little Italian guy floored us all when he came back to work. People want to put on his gravestone RIP. I think it should be DNR. I am waiting for him to visit with me in spirit.

CONTENTS

1. A Fortunate Life 9
2. The Show Must Go On 36
3. A Passion for Passions 59
4. An Emotional Appeal 85
5. The Basic Ingredients: Health
    and (Some) Wealth 110
6. My Curious Quest for
    Adventure 139
7. Working to Find Happiness . . . 163
8. Relationships Are Not All
    Relative 186
9. My Principal Beliefs 213
10. Where Does Time Go? 239

1.

A FORTUNATE LIFE

I have lived a fortunate life. I, literally and proverbially, have been to the mountaintop. I have met the most extraordinary people and enjoyed the most amazing experiences. I have ridden horses across prairies and motorcycles across the country. I have watched the miracle of my children growing into adulthood. I have lived the entire spectrum of emotions; I have felt tremendous joy and the deepest pain; I have loved and hated; I have gone to the extremes and savored passions. I have felt ecstasy. I was born in 1931; in my lifetime I have witnessed the discovery of antibiotics and the elimination of dreaded diseases, I have seen the inventions of television and the internet and the microwave; I have watched with awe the growth of commercial aviation as well as the NFL. Mine has been a life that has spanned eight decades of excitement and discovery and relationships and a lot of luck.

So I sure wasn't ready for it to end.

I have also seen death in its many forms. I have seen death in the natural order of things as my parents aged and died. I have seen the tragedy of accidental death as my wife died in a truly tragic event. I have seen the close and painful death from disease of my close friends. I have held my dying animals in my arms as their life slipped away. I have felt the pain of loss, the emptiness. I have attended more funerals than I can count; I have searched for the right words to console countless bereaved people. I have wandered aimlessly trying to comprehend death, realizing I could never understand it. But in 2016 I had an entirely different encounter with death.

I was told by a doctor I had a terminal disease. That I was going to die.

Wait a second. This was something completely different. I had gotten very good at being sympathetic; I was the one who always went home at the end of the funeral. I didn't know how to react to this news. This truly was my funeral we were talking about.

"You have cancer," the doctor told me.

There must be some mistake, I thought. This is what happens to other people. This diagnosis was the end result of a chain beginning with my curiosity. While reading a magazine, I had learned that researchers had discovered that cancer cells give off a protein that essentially announces their presence. Scientists had developed a test that can search out this protein. It is an extremely sensitive test. My wife, Elizabeth, and I decided to take this test. When it revealed that she had cervical cancer, we went through a month of near hysteria, but other doctors ran more thorough tests and found nothing. That test was too sensitive, they told us.

And then I was diagnosed with prostate cancer. Me! My regular doctor explained that prostate cancer sometimes is very aggressive and sometimes is so benign you'll die of something else long before it kills you. Kills me? That couldn't be happening. To find out which type it was, he took my PSA, a marker for this disease. Until then it had been at one or two, well within safe limits. "It's ten," he reported. "That is an aggressive cancer." Ten! My body had betrayed me.

I have always felt like the great comedian George Burns, who lived to one hundred: I couldn't die as long as I was booked. And my schedule was too busy for me to find the time to die. On an intellectual level, I understood my prognosis; I had made out my will, which said that when I died this person got this, that person got that. But on an emotional level, I was certain I was never going to die. I denied it. To me, it was make out my will, then have a nice piece of strudel. Death didn't apply to me.

I remember noticing in the last few years that when I made personal appearances more and more people were asking more frequently and passionately for my autograph. I knew what that meant: They were expecting me to die soon and my autograph was suddenly going to become more valuable. Boy, I thought, am I going to fool them!

My initial reactions to the diagnosis were, I suppose, quite common: denial, fear, anger — as well as a dose of being insulted. I am in my eighties; I have lived a long life, but I certainly wasn't ready for it to end. I decided I wasn't going gentle into that good night. I was going to fight. I had new horses arriving and I had to ride them. I had personal appearances scheduled and my one-man show to do and I couldn't let down the audience. I was going to make a movie. And I was supported in a sea of love: my wife, children, my grandchildren. I have always believed there is a force that burns inside all of us, a burning desire to live that permeates all our cells, and I tried to ignite that. I tried to find the trigger to put my immune system in superkill mode. I don't have any idea if it helped or not, but I believed my immune system got fired up! I was not going to die easily.

Then I read that in certain cases testosterone supplements might have something to do with prostate cancer. I was taking them. I asked my doctor if I should stop taking the supplements. "Yeah," he agreed, "that would be a good idea."

I stopped. Three months later I took another PSA test. It had gone down to one. One. The doctor guessed that the testosterone had resulted in the elevated PSA level. I didn't bother taking the sensitive test. As the cancer specialists explained to Elizabeth and me, we get cancer cells all the time and usually your body eats them up. Your killer cells, T cells, attack and destroy them. The body gets cancer all the time and eliminates it, but that test is so sensitive it picked up the hint of it and combined with the PSA reading convinced me I was dying.

And while I was sorry to disappoint all of those people with my autograph, I was thrilled to learn I did not have cancer. I'm back to not dying. At least right away.

But during those three months I was living with my death sentence, I spent considerable time thinking about my life, about the lessons I've learned, the places I've been, the miracles I've seen, all of those encounters and events and experiences that have been wrapped together into one great burst of energy called life. And based on that I *want* to share with you, for the first time, my secret to live a good, long life:

Don't die.

That's it; that's the secret. Simply keep living and try not to slow down.

Many people have shared their secrets to a long and happy life. Do this; don't do that. Eat pickles. Don't eat pickles. And every one of them has worked — for them. Other people have passed along the wisdom they have gained. Meditate. Don't hold in your anger. Treat people as you want to be treated — unless you don't like somebody; then treat him or her differently. It all works; none of it works. In these pages I am going to tell you about those things that have worked for me, that have enriched my life or taught me lessons that made a difference. But here is the first of those lessons: One size doesn't fit all.

When people come to me and ask for advice, assuming I must have learned something vitally important in my lifetime, I respond with the best possible advice: Don't follow my advice. Each one of us is unique. Different. Not the same. You didn't have my mother. No one else can walk in my shoes; most people can't even fit into them. I can't wear your shoes; they make my bunions pinch. But why try? We each bring to every day an entirely different set of experiences and a unique personal point of view. We each see life through a different prism. We are physically, emotionally, and mentally different. We think and see and feel the same things differently. The breeze, the sensation of putting oil on my skin, the anger I feel when some driver cuts me off, my response to a joke or a movie — it's different, all of it.

For me, really for anyone, to try to tell anyone else how to live their life is the ultimate in hubris. There is no one way, or right way, to do anything. Is there only one path up a mountain? Is there only one way to maintain your health? Is there only one way to have a relationship, or are there many and they vary depending on whose shoes you have on your feet? I don't have those answers; maybe the holy men on the top of the mountain do. But they're living on top of a mountain; what could they possibly know about responding to a jerk who cuts you off when you're driving to Starbucks to get that first cup of morning coffee? Is there such a thing as mountain path rage? The point I'm making is that I am not a font of wisdom. I'm the guy who saved the Starship *Enterprise* for seventy-nine weeks and ended up kissing James Spader on a patio. I'm still asking the questions. Even at my age I am still trying to figure out how to make this strange, wonderful, bizarre thing called life work best. I do know what has worked for me and I'm pleased to be able to share it. Take from it what it's worth — which in real terms is the price of this book, less the discount.

I have enjoyed incredible fortune in my life and I have had opportunities that few other people have enjoyed. What I believe is we should all be gathering knowledge, as much knowledge as we can, like prehistoric man gathered food, and from that huge pile sift and use those things that make sense to our own lives.

With age supposedly comes wisdom. I read that a long time ago. But I am now deep into my eighties and I can with some sadness admit that I know very little. I have gained only enough wisdom to dismiss the belief that wisdom comes with aging. With aging, mostly, comes aches and pains. At times I feel as uninformed as I felt when I left the city and went out into the country for the first time in my life. I had grown up in Montreal, a great city of bright lights. In a city it's almost impossible to see the fullness of the night sky. But when I was eleven years old I was sent to a camp for children who didn't have a lot of money. I wandered out of my bunk one night and sat on a log and looked up, and for the first time I saw the enormity of the universe. I literally looked up and up until I fell over backward, overwhelmed by the vastness. I had no idea, no concept. I don't think I have ever lost that awe, or the desire to understand more about it than I do. I have spent my life searching for those answers, and I am still on the job. The only thing of which I am certain is that those people who make a living telling others that they have the answer don't have the answer.

Change is the only thing we can predict with confidence. What you know for certain, those things on which you base your decisions, are going to change. We are told to eat a lot of carbs and few proteins, but just a few years ago we were told the opposite. Avoid fats, the experts told us; now we're told some fats are healthy. Einstein told us the speed of light is exact, and that will never change, but who knows? Someone may find the speed of light varies. We've just discovered that there is a wobble in the gravitational center of Earth and it affects everything. Years ago people confidently planned for their future, picking a profession and studying for it and working hard at it only to discover years later that this profession no longer existed. Technology had replaced it. The path that people had pursued so diligently and in many cases had become expert, had come to a dead end. Even the greatest typewriter repairman in history became obsolete with the availability of the computer. For survival, it became necessary to change.

If I do have any wisdom at all it is limited to the area of my own experiences. For me, the best that I can do is reminisce about what I have learned and allow you to choose those things that may apply to you. That's really all I have to offer. Here's what happened, here's what I did, and here's how it turned out. I can't teach you; I can only say this was what worked — or in some cases didn't work — for me.

There has been some advice that made an impact on me. Someone, I'm not even certain who it was, told me once, "You have the career that is your career. It is the career that you deserve. It is, in effect, your journey in life and . . ." My career? My career and my plans have always been dependent on the next phone call. And I never knew when — or even if — the phone was going to ring. We are under the illusion that we choose our path, but we don't. The road isn't even paved. The road is being tarred as we go along. Those big rollers are just ahead of you and you walk along the road that you think you have chosen, but in effect you have little control over your life. Circumstances visit and you go along. You follow the winding road, you make some choices, but for the most part we are dependent on factors not under our control. Things happen. I never thought I would be an actor. I never thought I would make albums or write books. I never thought I would make speeches on subjects I had to research. All the various things that I have done — the acting, the traveling, the music, the books, the horses and motorcycles — all were not things I dreamt of doing. The opportunities presented themselves and I embraced them.

We are all called upon to make significant and often life-changing choices, and when that becomes necessary we spend a great deal of time wondering and worrying and pondering, trying to figure out all the angles, trying to make certain we make the best choice. This job or that job? Marry this man or woman or not? Accept this offer? Which is the choice that will lead to riches or happiness? Which one will lead to doom and decay? Here is one thing I've learned: There is no such thing as the best choice. There is no sure thing. There simply is no way of knowing what fate has in store for each of us.

I remember being at one of the crossroads of my life and having to make a decision. After I finished *Star Trek,* my career hit what actors refer to as a "respite," a brief lull, but what it actually means is you can't get a job. So I started working in summer stock. I traveled in a truck with my dog. I had put a shell on the truck bed, it was a sort of crawl-in cottage, and when I reached the next theater, rather than spending money on a hotel or motel, I would park my truck in the back of the parking lot, hook it up to an electrical supply, and live there for the run. I did that for three years.

When the season ended in September, I drove home to Los Angeles. We finished the second summer in Boston, and I took off, intending to drive cross-country in time to be home to celebrate the Jewish holidays with my three daughters. Sometime on the first day I stopped and did what every actor did every day — I called my agent. Just in case. This was long before cell phones, so I called him from a pay phone in a rest area. "Big news," he told me. "Rose Kennedy wants to invite you to a party at the Kennedy compound. Turn around and drive back to Boston. . . ."

The Kennedys wanted to invite me to a party? On the one hand, that was a big deal. I had no idea who else would be there. But on the other hand, I desperately wanted to see my kids. I was really torn, but finally I told him, "I can't make it; I've got to get home to see my kids." His best efforts to convince me failed.

I called him again two days later from Arizona. "Rose Kennedy's office called. They really want you at that party, Bill. They said they would send an airplane to pick you up, then fly you home."

The Kennedys were the most powerful family in the country. They were well connected in Hollywood. What I should have said was "I'm in Arizona. Get the plane here and we'll fly to L.A. to pick up my kids and I'll take my kids to the party."

That's what I should have said. What I did say was "I have to get home to my kids." I had a choice and I made it. When I got home, my children were absolutely thrilled to see me. I remember their exact words: "Oh, hi, Daddy. We're going to go out and play now."

Who knows what might have happened if I had made a different choice and attended the Kennedy party? I might have met a producer there who realized I was the actor he had been searching for and immediately cast me into his big-budget extravaganza. And then that movie tanked and I never got another job again instead of working steadily and having a long and successful career.

I have spent my life being an actor. Is there a less predictable profession? The road is often being laid just one day ahead of you; there are times you have to live in the back of a truck with your dog and wait for the road to catch up. In the 1960s, one of the great radio and TV writers, Norman Corwin, was commissioned by the University of Utah to write a play. I had performed in a number of TV programs he'd written. He wrote a wonderful play and told me he had written it with me in mind. It was extremely flattering. It was a beautiful play and I did it in Salt Lake City. I remember meeting a professor of Shakespeare at the university and inviting him to see the play, telling him that there were passages in it the equal of

Shakespeare. He scoffed at that — until he saw the play. Then he told me that "there were moments that had the poetry and gravitas of Shakespeare." The play was very well received and it appeared it was going to move to Broadway. Just about then I got a phone call telling me the pilot I had made for a TV series called *Star Trek* had sold. What if I had gone to Broadway instead of taking that job? There was no way for me, or for anyone, to have predicted what would happen. I could have spent days and weeks and months pondering every element of that decision and it would have made no difference.

I have led a fortunate existence. I have been in the right place at the right time, which generally is better than making the "right" choice. I have gotten parts that called for the character to be young and handsome (at least I was young) who could say the words realistically enough but also had to have a look in the eyes, because the camera considered the eyes. I had the right color eyes and Paul Newman wasn't available. Or the girl had the right look, she had the necessary voluptuousness, and gave off such amazing pheromones that she could a build a career on it until she no longer gave off the same attractiveness. Talent matters, talent matters a great deal, but only if the phone rings.

The most amazing aspect of my life, of my career, is that the phone rang at the right time. Unusual things have always happened to me; that path was being laid for me. When I needed a job, the phone would ring with an offer. When there was a problem, a solution would occur. During an autograph session several years ago, someone on the line gifted me with a lovely bottle of wine. And then, later on that line, someone else gave me a corkscrew. Why did that happen? Who brings a corkscrew to an autograph session? But it did happen; it did. I have learned to accept those mysteries and to appreciate them. But I still wonder, Why? I wonder if there is a pattern to my life that I haven't seen. I do know with certainty that there is far more in this world than I can understand. There is a world beyond the known world. I've seen that; I have seen the future become the present and then the past. I have seen the toys of *Star Trek* become the tools of everyday life. My life has spanned from the marvels of radio to the wonders of performing holograms. I know that I am endlessly intrigued by those things I don't know. But I do know there is more.

I am at an age when I can look back on my life and see the things that really mattered, those things that made a difference, and those that, while seemingly important at the time, had absolutely no impact on my life. It is both surprising and odd to look back over all those years and see which events mattered.

We are, all of us, the direct result of our childhood. Few people ever outgrow the events that shaped us. Somewhere deep inside each of us those childhood feelings continue to exist, and we spend our lives protecting them. The choices we make, the decisions we make, can most often be traced directly to those events. It is amazing to me those things that I remember. If I want to remember certain events or people, I can, but those aren't the events that have made such an enormous impact on my life. Just pause here for a minute, lean back, and think about your earliest childhood memories. The first thoughts that pop into your mind. Don't try to analyze them or direct your thoughts. Just close your eyes and enjoy the show.

The thread that has run through my life is loneliness. Even as a child I was never part of a group. I don't know why. It was not by choice. Maybe because I was Jewish in a predominantly non-Jewish school. But I was fighting all the time. I had very few friends. When I walked the ten blocks to school, I would see everybody else walking in a group. I was by myself. I wanted so much to be wanted. When I was in fifth grade, the class celebrated Valentine's Day by sending valentines to as many people as we wanted to. If you were sweet on a girl, you would send one to her. You might send one to a friend on the football team telling him it was nice to be on same team. I sent six valentines to myself so I would not be humiliated by receiving no valentines. Those were the only six valentines I received. It seems like such a small thing, yet I have never forgotten. I have never forgotten that terrible feeling of being so alone and so desperate to be part of the group. Loneliness was the hell that I lived in as a child.

That has extended to my whole life. I have had many acquaintances, there have been people I have cared about, but I have had very few friends. My closest friend was Leonard Nimoy. We were born four days apart and raised in Orthodox Jewish homes. We shared so much throughout our careers. I loved Leonard, and he used to refer to me as his brother. Yet at the end of his life and for reasons I still don't know, he was not my friend. I would call him and he wouldn't answer the phone or return any messages. He died and I didn't feel welcome at his funeral. The only people who really have known me were my four wives, and with each of them I had a very different relationship.

The second memory from my childhood that has resonated throughout my life concerns my mother. Oh, here we ago, another Jewish kid with mother issues. But I will go to my death remembering one moment — not simply remembering the words but also remembering the feeling. How casual and innocent it was in that moment, and the implications were an earthquake in my personality. I was no more than seven years old. I remember it so well. I was sitting in the breakfast nook, sunlight was streaming into the room, and she was to my right. I asked the question that every boy probably asks his mother: "Who do you love more, me or Daddy?"

She didn't even hesitate: "Daddy, because he gives me things."

And thus psychiatry was born! Believe me, all the psychiatrists in the world couldn't have put me together again after that. My relationships with women for much of the rest of my life might all be traced to that day. I lived at home until I graduated from McGill University. I was twenty-one years old. I can't remember great moments, I can't remember bad moments, but that one moment with my mother remains blazing in my head.

I enjoy watching sports and I often hear athletes at the height of their glory speaking about their mothers in such loving terms: "I'm dedicating this to you, because you were always there." And when I hear that there's the feeling of emptiness again. I never felt that way. I never felt that my mother was always there.

There was a time when I tried to fill that sense of loneliness with a woman. I remember the first time I asked a woman to marry me. There was a group at the university that put on plays, including musicals. It was the only group that I was part of in college. I would act or write or even direct some of them. There was a beautiful student assistant who also was a member. She was pretty and sweet, and we started dating. She lived in New York. I went to visit her there and we took a walk in Central Park and I asked her to marry me. I know exactly why I did that: I just didn't want to be alone. I didn't have the slightest idea what being married meant. She seemed like a nice person, she was pretty, why not marry her? Fortunately, she said no.

I have been married four times. I have spent my life seeking love. The absence of love has been the major force of my life. When there was a vacuum, it needed to be filled. The women may have changed from time to time, but the need to be married never went away. The need to have someone at my home, waiting for me, wanting me to be home.

I retained an image in my mind of a lighted window. That window represents everything I have been seeking. I was always driving a car or riding on a train, looking at a house in the distance with a lighted window. Maybe the lamp was near the window; the light was amber and yellow. The window was clear and the house was comfortable looking. That lighted window was home, warmth, and love. There was love inside that room. There were arms around you. The meals were served to you to say how much someone was loved. There was a bed and there was passion. All of it was on the other side of that window.

Every journey I took, whether it was for a day or a year, I was looking for that window.

And it was always in the distance.

There were times I saw a window that looked inviting, and I would think, God, if I could just drive up there and knock on the door and say, "Can I stay here for a while?" How many times have I thought there might be someone who would say, "Hey, it's Bill Shatner; come in and let me put my arms around you"? I spent much of my life settling for much less. I wonder how many times — at the height of my fame — I drove past a hotel on my way to an unhappy home and thought, if I could hide there in that hotel, if I could be anonymous and stay there, then I might be happy.

But I needed to have my dogs there with me. So I would make my way back to another unhappy home and live my unhappy life until it dissolved and became another life.

I learned that simply being married wasn't enough. In my first marriage I had that lighted window. I had a woman who loved me, and we had three beautiful babies whom I nurtured and loved. It was everything that I had dreamt of — and it was being destroyed by a series of circumstances that I didn't understand and couldn't help. It wasn't enough. I had no control of it. I was not a good husband. I certainly had a lot to learn. I was so unhappy in my first marriage that things got terribly out of hand. And it was my fault.

For so many years I had to stand in front of the camera and be somebody else. While doing *Star Trek,* I had to carry on with effortless command and be a convincing actor. I had to stand in front of the camera and lie. Well, I did it. I was convincing people I had some control over my own life, that I was making decisions. After *Star Trek* became a cult hit and we all started getting more attention than any of us imagined possible, some of my cast mates complained that I was aloof. "Shatner is too big or too good for us."

That was never true. I didn't know how to be any different. I didn't know how to be a friend. In reality, I was a frightened child who was losing everything that meant comfort.

When I reach back into my childhood, a third memory emerges that also has made a significant difference throughout my entire life. We lived on the west end of Montreal, which at the time was an English-speaking section. But it truly was the end of the city, so much so that only a block or two away there was a stable that rented riding horses by the hour. People would ride those horses through the farmers' fields that surrounded the area. I was ten or eleven years old, and I desperately wanted to ride. I had never been on a horse in my life; as far as I was aware, no one in my family had ridden. My father made cheap suits; he didn't ride horses. My mother worried about looking good, so the thought of her being on a horse is ludicrous. The story I tell is that I cleaned out the stables to earn enough money to rent a horse for an hour, but I don't think that is completely true. But somehow I got the money and rented a horse. In my memory I was by myself, but I don't see how that can be true. I don't think they would have allowed a child who had never been on a horse to go out by himself. It's sketchy, but in this memory I was in the fields walking along and cantering. At the end of the hour my parents showed up, and I galloped into their presence and I reined in the horse.

That is absolutely true. My mother asked, and these were her words, "Where did you learn how to do that?" I think I responded, "I have been doing it for years." Which wasn't true, of course, although in my mind I had been doing it for years. I don't know why I have the affinity for horses, but throughout my life that has been the one place I have gone that provided solace. I'm a city kid, a guy from Montreal; why is it that I find peace riding a horse?

Horses have also been a continuing thread of my life. Riding them and, when I was financially able, owning them and breeding them. At the worst moments of my life I turned to my horses to find a semblance of peace. After my third wife, Nerine, drowned in our swimming pool, I was twisted in grief. I was completely lost. Nerine was an alcoholic and I had failed to save her. Within two or three days following her death I drove out to the stable. I got on a horse and sat there in the corner of the corral and wept. It is a vivid memory. I walked the horse through the afternoon, my tears just flowing. Day after day, I drove forty-five miles to the farm, sat on my horse, and cried. For a long time the only consolation I had was getting on a horse.

When I am on a horse I am completely in that moment. For my own safety, for the safety of the horse, I have to be right there. My mind can't be wandering, and so for those hours I was on a horse I had at least a partial escape from my pain. I also have gotten tremendous joy from my horses. I met my present wife, Elizabeth, who was a trainer, through our mutual love of horses. I have seen the value of horses as therapy animals and have spent decades of my life hosting the Hollywood Charity Horse Show, raising millions of dollars for special-needs children.

I have many other memories from my childhood — people and places, the excitement of being on a stage and getting approval — but none of them has the emotional impact of these three events: being so lonely I sent myself the only valentines I received, being told by my mother she loved my father more than me because he gave her things, and being able to ride a horse. At the time each of them took place it never would have occurred to me that more than seventy-five years later they still would be resonating emotionally.

We all have experienced events like these, and they have shaped us no less than a million years of winds and rivers have formed the Grand Canyon. Those are mine; those are the things that I have been responding to in one way or another for a lifetime. They are unique to me, as each individual has his or her own particular memories. But it's worth trying to figure out which events from your childhood are your emotional anchors. Because so many of the important decisions that we all make as we go through life are in response to those events.

I know my own failings, and I admit them.

I have not always been the man I wanted to be. But I have learned some important lessons in all my years as I stumbled through life to success and, even, incredibly as I have to admit, to happiness. Take of it what you will. Use those parts of it that make sense to you. This is the bounty of my life, the sum of my experience.

2.
THE SHOW MUST GO ON

In December 1970, a year after we had finished shooting the third and final season of *Star Trek* but before it became a cultural phenomenon, I was cast into a new play by a young writer named Mart Crowley. Mart Crowley would later write the magnificent play *The Boys in the Band.* This was not that play; it was titled *Remote Asylum.* I played a "physically and spiritually exhausted American" tennis pro. A lovely woman named Nancy Kelly played my "cosmopolitan, not-yet-divorced lover." The play opened at the Ahmanson Theatre in L.A., which was where we would work out any problems on our way to Broadway.

The play opened with Nancy Kelly and me standing in the darkness saying our opening lines. Then the lights went on and the curtain went up. We had been rehearsing for several weeks. It was a complicated play; the setting was a beautiful Mediterranean villa, which, we will discover, is not a paradise but rather "an inferno where a painful, purgatorial breakthrough occurs."

On opening night, as we were standing there in the darkness waiting for our cue to begin, Nancy leaned over and whispered those words every actor dreads hearing: "Are we in a disaster?"

Actually, the "painful, purgatorial breakthrough" was the play. We may have suspected it while we were in rehearsals, but we persevered. We did our jobs. The play ran one night.

The reality is actors rarely know if the play or movie or TV pilot they are making is going to be a success or a dismal failure. I have experienced every variation of that; I know enough to know how little I know. I starred in the only full-length movie ever made in Esperanto, the universal language. It was a foreign film in every country in the world. By the time the film was released, I had forgotten the language and even I didn't understand what it was about. But when we were making it, I worked as hard on it as anything else I have ever done. I didn't allow my doubts about the quality or the potential to influence my work ethic at all. I showed up and I did my job.

Any success I have had began by my

showing up on time, being prepared, and doing the best possible job.

There is a lot to be said for that. That isn't wisdom; that's common sense. But in my life, it has made all the difference. "The show must go on" is the actor's credo, but it can just as easily be applied to anything you do. A good work ethic is the foundation of success. Show up on time prepared to do your job.

I don't know how not to work. My work ethic is ingrained in me. Working, I have always found, led directly to more work. There is little in life more frightening to me than blank pages in my datebook.

I don't know precisely when I became obsessed with work. But I am. In January 2016, I was eighty-four years old and was on tour with my one-man show. I was doing eight shows in eight cities in eight nights. I was traveling with one person, Lucky Dave Memory, who was my stage manager and problem solver. We landed at Newark Airport on Thursday night and the following morning we rented a little Fiat to drive to the Westbury Music Fair on Long Island for a show that night. Saturday morning we were scheduled to fly out of LaGuardia to Chicago for a performance at the Rialto Square Theatre in Joliet, Illinois.

On Friday morning, Lucky Dave got in the passenger seat and I drove. I love to drive, but I had never driven a Fiat before. We had a little bit of luggage that barely fit in the trunk. While we were driving to Long Island, we heard the first reports about a major snowstorm heading up the coast from Washington. They were forecasting as much as three feet of snow farther south — although at first they predicted New York would get only three inches. I was concerned but not worried. By the time we got to Westbury, the forecast had been increased to six to eight inches. By late afternoon, it had turned into "a snow event" that might dump as much as three feet of snow on the metropolitan area.

Meanwhile, I've got to do my show on Long Island and get to Illinois.

The storm was scheduled to hit New York around midnight. If my show ended on time, I could get to LaGuardia Airport and get a flight to Chicago before it started snowing, and from there I would go to Joliet. My assistant, the tour manager, Kathleen Hays, was doing everything possible to make reservations. We were all set — and then at four o'clock, LaGuardia, JFK, and Newark were closed. I called Kathleen. "What about Hartford?" I said. "Hartford never closes." It turned out Hartford did have a flight to Chicago, but it made two stops and took six hours. Book it. I didn't care. I had a show to do.

By eight o'clock, Hartford was closed. Lucky Dave asked me, "Now what are we going to do?"

I looked him in the eye. Lucky Dave is an adventurous soul. We discovered we were thinking the same thing: We have to drive it.

Let me review: I was eighty-four years old. My bills were all paid and there was more money in the bank than I would ever spend. The theater manager from Joliet had called Kathleen and told her he would understand if we had to cancel. There literally was no compelling reason that I had to get there.

It never seriously occurred to me to cancel the show. I was booked. The show had to go on. I'd spent seven decades showing up on time and prepared. Something inside me whispered that the day I stopped showing up was the day I started dying. Lucky Dave told me, "A friend of mine is coming to the show tonight. He weighs more than two hundred pounds. He can sit in the back." Lucky Dave then reminded me he was a New Yorker and didn't have a driver's license, but his friend, Big Pete, would spell me behind the wheel.

Okay, we had a plan. No one said it was a good plan, but it was a plan. When the show ended at ten o'clock, we were going to get into a small four-wheel-drive Fiat and attempt to outrace the snowstorm.

The show started late because of the impending storm. By the time I finished the usual meet and greet and signed some autographs, it was almost eleven o'clock. We threw everything into the car. Lucky Dave got in the passenger seat. Big Pete squeezed into the back. We took off! I was determined: "If we can just get over the George Washington Bridge before it starts snowing . . ."

We made it over the bridge and onto the Jersey Turnpike. I was totally focused. At that moment there was nothing in my life more important than making it to Joliet in time to perform my one-man show. I was obsessed. I had to get there. We made it to US 80, still no snow. And then, just after midnight, I saw the first snowflakes in my headlights.

We were in Pennsylvania when the blizzard really hit. I could barely see ahead of me. Most of the traffic were very large trucks, which raced by me going seventy, eighty miles an hour. From the back, Big Pete finally admitted, "I don't know how to drive in snow."

It didn't matter. I was the commander of this ship and I was taking us to Illinois. I was from Montreal. I had learned to drive in snow. Of course, living in California for the past five decades hadn't provided a lot of opportunity to practice. I decided I would get behind a truck and let it clear my path. I found a truck going a reasonable speed and tucked in behind it.

Conditions were getting worse. There were at least six inches of snow on the road, which was beginning to ice up. I stayed about forty yards behind the truck, which suddenly moved over to a side lane — and directly in front of me was a silver Audi, stopped in the middle of the icy highway. I managed to ease over and just missed hitting him. As I went past the stalled Audi, I saw it was turned around, pointing directly at us, and all its lights were on — blinkers, brake lights, it was all lit up. I glanced at Lucky Dave. He was staring straight ahead, his eyes opened wider than I had ever seen.

We kept going. I was driving as if my life depended on getting to Joliet, which, as we were experiencing, it actually did. We continued for another hour, then decided to stop for gas and sustenance. We had been passing rest areas and I had noticed that the large trucks were huddled there, like rows of elephants, waiting for this blinding snowstorm to let up. I finally pulled into one of the rest areas. As Big Pete went into the McDonald's, I began tracking the storm on my cell phone. Fifty miles ahead of us there still was a hundred percent chance of snow, but thirty miles beyond that there was only a 90 percent chance.

"There's an opening!" I shouted to Lucky Dave and Big Pete. A 10 percent chance seemed like quite a bit at that moment. We jumped back in the car and took off. We got back on the highway and settled in. And no more than seven or eight minutes later, there, stopped right in the middle of the road, was the silver Audi. I steered around him again, and this time the brakes locked up. Somehow we slid right past him. "That's the ghost Audi," I said. It was incredible. I had been going fifty miles an hour or more for at least two hours. We had stopped for no more than ten minutes. How could it possibly have gotten ahead of us? There was no rational explanation, but there it was.

It began snowing harder. I just kept going. What we were doing made no sense. I knew that, but I couldn't help myself. There was no one else on the road; the biggest trucks had pulled to the side. I kept going. I was terrified we were going to slide off the road into a snowbank. We didn't have anything we might need with us; we didn't even have a blanket. Big Pete finally spoke up, suggesting that maybe it made sense to stop in a rest area.

Sense? Stop? "I have to get to Joliet," I said, my eyes focused on whatever road I could see.

As we got to the 90 percent area, the snow seemed to slow. Then we got to 80 percent. And boom, we drove out of the storm.

We reached Joliet in the morning. I slept several hours and did a performance. No one seemed to care that I had risked my life to get to Joliet. They had paid their money for tickets and they wanted to be entertained.

After the show, I had planned to get some sleep, but I was so wound up that it was impossible. We got into the Fiat, Big Pete crawled into the back, and we drove directly to Detroit. I dropped Big Pete at the airport, and he flew back to New York. I did the show in Detroit that night and the next day I flew home.

How foolish I was. Three guys in a Fiat 500? What drove me to do it? Well, certainly not Big Pete, as he didn't drive at all.

The lesson that has made a difference in my life is that success always begins with showing up. I think it is accurate to state that not every show or movie in which I appeared could be considered prestigious. I give a great deal of thought to turning down anything; instead I see each job as an opportunity to practice my craft — and get paid for doing it. I have to admit when I accepted was the role of "the TV producer" in the 1982 film *Visiting Hours,* the story of "a deranged, misogynistic killer who assaults a journalist. When he discovers that she survived the attack, he follows her to the hospital to finish her off." I didn't expect to receive critical acclaim. I expected to do my job to the best of my ability, get my paycheck, and then, I hoped, get another job.

It was a job and I accepted it. I showed up. I chased the killer through the halls of the hospital.

There is a story I heard a long time ago that has stuck with me. Very few people know that young John Wayne was one of the first singing cowboys. Wayne made a series of B Westerns. They cost almost nothing, they had very little plot beyond the guy in the white hat beating up the guy in the black hat, and they had to be shot in six days. Apparently one day during the Depression he was walking on the Fox lot and ran into the great humorist Will Rogers. "How's it going, kid?" Rogers asked him.

In response, Wayne released all his frustrations, complaining that the studio had him making terrible B movies, they had him singing songs; he went on and on.

Rogers listened patiently, and when Wayne finally calmed down he gave him the best advice Wayne ever received. "You working?" he asked.

Wayne nodded. "Yeah."

"Keep working," he said, and walked away.

That really sums up what I believe: Keep working. Show up and do your job and good things are going to happen. And sometimes that means doing your job under less than ideal circumstances.

An actor is most often entirely dependent on the decisions of other people to keep working. And the reality is that the older you get in this business, the more difficult it becomes to find roles. At some point in every actor's career, casting agents begin looking for a "William Shatner type," for example, because William Shatner can no longer play William Shatner. But if you're extraordinarily fortunate, as I have been, you become so well known that people continue to enjoy your work. In order to fill those blank pages on my schedule, I created my one-man show. It's performance art. I wrote the show and I helped create the staging. I take the show on the road for a week or more several times a year. I like to refer to it as William Shatner Without the Dancing Girls.

It's just me, onstage for almost two hours. My friend Brad Paisley wrote a song that includes the lyric "I'm an entertainer, and that's all." That's the object of my show: Let me entertain for ninety minutes. I tell some stories; I sing a few songs; I schmooze. When I first started doing the show, I was onstage with another person. I usually recruited a well-known DJ from a local radio station to sit opposite me and ask questions. But when I was invited to perform the show at the Music Box Theatre on Broadway, I changed the structure. I eliminated the questions and replaced the other person with a chair. The rolling chair becomes my prop: It's my motorcycle, it's my horse, it's a Fiat 500 with an imaginary Big Pete stuffed into the backseat — but I also need it so I can sit down for a few minutes.

The prospect of opening on Broadway fifty years after my last appearance was thrilling to me. New York audiences are the most demanding, the most critical, and the most loving — so I rewrote my show and restaged it in preparation for this appearance. I added material; I took out material; essentially it was a new show, and I was doing it for the first time on opening night.

I was extremely anxious. I wondered, What the hell are they going to think? The night before my opening, Elizabeth and I and my manager, Larry Thompson, had an early dinner, so I could get to bed and be well rested for my performance. I had a simple hamburger in a very good restaurant. I awoke the next morning with food poisoning.

My stomach was dancing. I felt deathly ill. I spent the entire day in my hotel room. I didn't dare move more than a few feet away from the bathroom. The amazing Dr. Mehmet Oz came to my hotel room to help me. I was completely dehydrated, but I couldn't keep anything down. I was sick and I was weak. But there was never any consideration of canceling the show. I was doing a one-man show on Broadway. I had been preparing for this night for fifty years.

I finally made it to the theater. The Music Box was sold out, the critics were in their seats, and I was suffering from food poisoning. I walked out onstage into the warmth of an audience. It was the best possible medicine. As I began the show, my fears disappeared and, for a few minutes, so did my food poisoning. I forgot all about it — for a short time. And then it hit me again.

I was surprised to discover I had anything left inside me. But about halfway through the show, I crapped in my pants. Everything I had learned, everything I believed about the show going on, was tested that night. I remember standing onstage thinking, Someday I will tell this story from a historical point of view and people will laugh at my embarrassment. It will make a wonderful story — but not tonight. Not right now.

I told the audience, "I'm sorry, but we've had a slight technical difficulty. I will be right back." I ran upstairs and took a quick shower. Elizabeth was there. I changed my pants and ran back downstairs and back onto the stage to finish the show. To my amazement, that was the last of it. The show received very good notices and I had no further problems for the remainder of my run. The show ran and my runs ended.

Showing up often requires simply saying yes. Someone I know lives by a standing rule: When the phone rings, the answer is "yes." It doesn't even matter what the question is: "Yes" is the answer. That also might be the actor's credo. Few actors, especially at the beginning, the middle, or the end of their careers, can afford to turn down an opportunity to work. Work leads to more work. "We want you to play a rock with feelings. Do you want me to be a boulder or a pebble?" "We want you to star in a movie being filmed in a language no one speaks"? *"Kie estas la necesejo?"* Which in Esperanto means either "I'll take the job" or "Where is the nearest toilet?" A producer I have often worked with and admired wanted to put me on top of a glacier by helicopter all by myself and then fly away. My two greatest fears are loneliness and heights, and this would combine both of them. "Yes," I said.

His last words to me as the helicopter took off, leaving me completely alone thousands of feet high in a mountain range, were, "Don't move around too much. There might be a crevasse close by."

Oh, the one thing he didn't have to worry about was my moving around too much.

Saying yes is a beginning, and by saying no or equivocating you cut yourself off from opportunity. It's like saying no to a blind date. That man or woman might not be the ideal person for you, but short of having dinner with a serial killer you are giving yourself an opportunity to see a new world, to meet new people, to have new adventures. Sometimes saying yes when logic and common sense tell you to say no does make

50

a significant difference. At the beginning of my career I was fortunate enough to be working for the great director Tyrone Guthrie at the Stratford Festival. It was a remarkable opportunity for a young actor to work with some of the finest actors of our time. I was a supporting actor, meaning I filled whatever small roles were available. When we did *Henry V* I played the small role of Duke of Gloucester, as well as understudying our leading man, Christopher Plummer.

I was onstage for about five minutes; Chris Plummer carried the show. This is one of the longest roles ever written by Shakespeare. It is a complex role that requires peeling away layers of a man's soul, and Chris Plummer was brilliant in it. He received rave reviews. But being diligent about my work, I studied the role. I was certain it was mostly a good learning opportunity, as these were limited-run productions and the leading man or woman almost never missed a performance. And because we were usually rehearsing the next play while performing in the current run, the understudies never had an opportunity to actually perform the role on a stage.

In fact, it required nothing less than death or an extremely painful kidney stone to prevent the leading actors from going on.

One morning shortly after we opened I received a call from the production office: Chris Plummer was in excruciating pain with a kidney stone. Could I go on that night?

Go onstage to replace one of the most respected young actors in the theater, performing one of Shakespeare's most complex roles in a play that I had never rehearsed? In fact, I had never said the lines out loud. I hadn't met some of the other actors. We hadn't had a single run-through, I didn't know if the costume fit. My entire preparation consisted of watching Plummer perform the role.

There really is only one correct answer to that question: "Absolutely!" I said yes, of course, definitely. I didn't know how to say no.

I did not even consider the risk I was taking. I was a young actor no one had ever heard of. I was courting disaster: My career could have ended that night. "Shatner? Isn't he that guy who made a fool of himself at the Stratford Festival?"

Looking back on this more than sixty years later, I have great admiration for that kid. I can't remember what I must have been thinking, but I am thrilled that I had the guts to say yes, even at that early point in my life. There are people who would have said no; clearly that was the sensible answer. But not me. This has been another of those threads that have run through my life. I say yes.

What I remember most about that night was the lack of fear that I felt. I should have been nervous. I was about to go onstage completely unrehearsed in front of a full house in one of the more prestigious theaters in the world. Why wasn't I terrified? Where did that confidence come from? Or was I simply so naïve I didn't know any better?

I did not know the staging, so my biggest concern was not knocking over any of the other actors. Knocking over actors during a performance is generally considered bad form. When a show opens, the director "freezes" it, meaning that the actors are supposed take the same actions and say the same lines the same way every performance. The slightest deviation causes a ripple effect, forcing every other actor to respond to it.

The night I went on for Christopher Plummer, my staging was pretty simple: When Plummer had sat down, I stood up; when he had stood up, I sat down. The performance went beautifully. It went extraordinarily well. The other actors were supportive; I could feel the audience rooting for me. I didn't miss a line or a cue — until one of the last scenes. As the French Princess entered, I looked directly at her and went blank. I knew I had a line, but I had no idea what it might be. ("Hi, Princess, how's it going?")

It was at that moment that I realized "yes" might not have been the right answer. I stood there in noble silence. I was in the middle of the actor's nightmare. Also in the cast was the fine young actor Don Cherry, who was playing my younger brother. Most important at that moment was the fact that Don Cherry had a photographic memory. He knew the entire play, word for word. I invented my own staging, and ignoring the French Princess, I walked over to Don Cherry and threw my arm over his shoulder and whispered, "What's the line?"

Don Cherry smiled but didn't have the slightest idea. But in that instant I remembered my line! I spoke it as if I had known it the whole time, and only the entire cast understood what had happened. I received a standing ovation and grand reviews. In many ways that night transformed me from a performer into an actor. It marked the real beginning of my professional career. At

Stratford I began getting larger roles, which led to other opportunities.

I said yes, and that made all the difference.

Admittedly there have been other times I said yes that might not have turned out so well. Earlier in my life, fifty years ago, I was a hunter. I can't imagine now how I could have found it acceptable to kill animals for sport, but I did. I was not one of those people who claim they need to hunt for food. I went to restaurants for food. I hunted for sport. Today I am philosophically, socially, morally, empirically against hunting. I haven't gone hunting in decades. But at that time I made several appearances on those outdoor hunting TV shows. The exposure was considered good for an actor's career.

I hunted with a bow and arrow. I was quite proficient. I actually competed in the Cobo Center in Detroit. But now I was invited to hunt wild pig on Catalina Island. "Yes," I said, of course. In this instance we did intend to eat the animal. I saw a wild pig and I launched an arrow and struck him. The wounded pig ran into the thick brush, creating a tunnel. I was with a guide, who was carrying a gun because a wild pig is a large and dangerous animal. It can kill a man. The guide said to me, "Here's what we are going to do. I'm going to circle around to the far end of the brush. When I'm in position, you go into the tunnel and flush him out the other side. I'll shoot him."

Once again it didn't occur to me to say no. This was all being filmed! Or, more logically, what I should have said was "I've got a good idea: *You* go in that tunnel and flush him out, and I'll wait on the other side and shoot him with my bow and arrow." Instead I said yes. I didn't think I had a choice.

I walked into that hole in the brush. It was so thick it was impossible to turn around. The only thing I could have done was back out or, if I were being chased by a wounded pig, run for my life out. It was so dense that the cameraman couldn't follow me in. Or perhaps, as I now think of it in retrospect decades later, the cameraman was too smart to follow me in. Instead he shot pictures of the brush moving. "You in there, Bill?"

"I'm in there."

"Okay, good. Keep going."

I did as instructed; I was in fifteen feet, twenty feet, when I suddenly realized I was trapped. I was in a tunnel and I couldn't get out. If that pig turned on me, as wounded animals will do, I was helpless. I was armed with a bow and arrow, which I couldn't lift up because the brush was too thick.

Fortunately, I had mortally wounded that animal, which died in the brush.

But the symbolism of that moment is very vivid to me. How many times I have been in shows in which I felt trapped and unable to get out? Shows in which the whole cast is wondering, What are we doing here?

I have had to make choices every day of my life. I have learned not to wait for some Divine Inspiration that suddenly is going to appear to tell me the right answer, the right road to follow. It hasn't happened yet. Instead I made a choice, and then I did everything I was capable of doing to make certain it proved to be the best possible choice for me. Life is cyclical, I've learned, and some of those choices I've made have been the right ones. And while I'll never know for certain, I'm quite sure some of those situations might have turned out better if I had made a different choice.

But as I look back on my life there isn't too much I would change about it. Those choices I made in my decades-long run, the right ones and the less right ones, turned out to have made very little difference taken as a whole. The important thing was to make the best of every decision and never look back on it.

There is one thing that has made a consistent difference thoughout my life: I said yes.

3.
A PASSION FOR PASSIONS

One evening in late April 2017, my wife, Elizabeth, and I went to our favorite Thai restaurant. The place doesn't look like much, it's in the back of a small mall, but I guarantee that it has absolutely the best Thai food you will ever eat. On our way to dinner I noticed one of the tires on our car needed air, so I stopped at what is literally the single best service station in the world, and without question the most brilliant attendant filled the tire with what was undoubtedly the finest air available anywhere on earth.

I've spent my life in the pursuit of passion. Passion is that . . . that thing, that stuff, which makes life worth living.

Here is another thing I've learned: Just living life isn't sufficient. That's not what life is supposed to be about. We have all been given this most extraordinary gift: We have been put on this planet for a span of years, and we need to do more with that time than mow the front lawn. Years ago Herb Gardner wrote a wonderful play, *A Thousand Clowns,* which then became a Jason Robards movie. It is the story of an iconoclast who is trying to teach his nephew the pursuit of passion. In one scene, as the iconoclast is trying to explain himself to a pretty social worker who believes his philosophy is a threat to his nephew, he tells her, "I want him to know the sneaky, subtle reason he was born a human being and not a chair."

We have to yearn for things, we have to pursue them, and if we are fortunate enough to obtain them we have to savor them — and then set off on the next pursuit. I have always been a man of great enthusiasms. When I find something I like, I have a desperate need to share it with everyone I know. Truthfully, I know that the Thai restaurant probably isn't the best Thai restaurant in the world, and that service station may only be the second or third best, and while the air was excellent there might be equally good air found in other places. But that doesn't really matter to me. I can be as enthusiastic about the *tom kha* coconut soup at Talésai on Ventura Boulevard as I can be about any entrée I've ever eaten.

And at that moment I mean it; I believe it.

I have gone through life finding and sharing my passions. There is a common mistake many people make: They equate passion solely with sex or with love. They are in endless pursuit of a "passionate romance" or a "passionate affair." Meaning they are desperate to feel a deep connection with another human being.

Certainly one place to find passion is in a relationship, but it is a shame to limit passion to that. The pursuit and enjoyment of passion, however the hell you want to define it, is what life should be about. When somebody asks you what it is you are searching for in life, your answer better be passion. By definition, passion is "the strongest of all emotions." It is "a strong feeling of enthusiasm or excitement," an "extravagant fondness, enthusiasm, or desire for anything."

As I explained, my search for passion with a woman has been the driving force of my life. I have found it; admittedly at times I found it in the wrong places and at the wrong times. But I was fortunate to have had many passionate encounters. Some of them were limited in duration and scope; others lasted for a considerable time. And I felt the amazing intensity, the extraordinary feeling that I was exploring the outer limits of my emotions. That it couldn't possibly get any better than this. This was it; this was what I had been searching for. I had reached the mountaintop.

Until the next time. The next mountain. I have great news for you: I can report to you from eighty-seven years old that no matter how passionate you are, you will never run out of it. There is no limited reservoir of passion. To this day, to this moment, I am still in the thrall of physical and emotional passion. You don't have to hold any of it in reserve until the right person or Thai restaurant comes along. No matter how much passion you display, there's a lot more where that came from — but only if you learn how to accept it and enjoy it.

Passion isn't sex — although sex certainly can be passionate. Passion also plays an important role in the pursuit of an attractive woman or man. The passion of the chase. That song is right: "The Things We Do for Love." The chase serves to heighten the passion, even if at times it is never more than a fantasy. And that feeling never goes away either.

So I know that physical passion. But I have seen and felt passion in so many other places. I often think of the amazing Christopher Reeve. I had met him briefly before the accident that turned him into a quadriplegic, though I certainly didn't know him. But I knew we shared a love of horses. The problem with Chris was that his upper body was so muscular he actually was a little top-heavy. Many horsemen think that made it difficult for him to stay perfectly balanced on a horse, which may have been a factor when he was thrown from his horse.

After his injury, because of our shared love of horses, I wanted to offer my support and express my sympathy. I made an appointment to see him in the rehabilitation facility. He was in New Jersey. I went to the facility, and as I walked through the glass doors I saw him sitting in his wheelchair waiting for me. He was being held upright and he had a breathing tube in his mouth. As I entered, I felt a sense of panic: It struck me that I was going to visit a man I barely knew. What in the world would we talk about? How awkward was this going to be?

The first thing I heard as I approached him was the battery-operated breathing mechanism pushing oxygen into his lungs. I was heartsick; this handsome, smart, vibrant young man reduced to depending on a device to breathe for him. There was a moment when I wondered, If this had happened to me, would I still want to live?

Air in, air expelled. I didn't know what to do. I was lost. I couldn't shake his hand. I couldn't ask "How are you?" Where to start, what to say? Chris solved that problem for me. His first words to me were "Tell me about your horses."

My horses? Well, of course. We spent the rest of my visit talking about our mutual love of horses. It would not be accurate to claim that I forgot his situation, I didn't, but it no longer was the center of our conversation. For more than an hour we were two guys who were passionate about horses talking about them. As he had asked, I told him about my horses, and he responded with stories of horses he had ridden and loved.

And as we did, I realized he was as passionate about horses as probably he had ever been, and that love certainly contributed to keeping him alive. He was never going to ride again, he knew that, but he was savoring the passion of the chase.

I have a list of passions, things that fulfill me, that remain central to my life. It doesn't matter what your passion is, as long as it exists. A life without passion is like a black-and-white movie; it lacks the potential richness. For me, my primary passion, like Chris Reeve's, is horses. The pursuit of that passion continues to fill my life.

I own horses; I ride horses; I breed horses. I have no idea why a city kid developed this passion for horses, but it is real. There is never a time when I am sitting on a horse that my life is not fuller. I have progressed in the course of my life from sitting on a horse and hoping I don't fall off to being something of a knowledgeable horseman. Riding well is a developed skill. The horse is a marvelous animal, able to express powerful physical emotion completely without intellect. Horses simply react to whatever is happening around them. They don't think; they don't filter information. They live entirely in the moment. They don't think, Geez, a lion almost got me yesterday, and they don't live in fear that the lion might return tomorrow. Instead they are thinking, I have to be alert right now; those bushes are moving; is there something there that might be dangerous to me? It's a wonderful lesson for us; wise men try to teach it all the time. We can't do anything about the past and we don't know what the future will bring, so there is nothing we can do but live in the moment. You can take that step or stand still.

That is what horses have taught me. But in return I am saying to them, through my commands, I will keep you safe. Do what I tell you to do and you have nothing to fear. A horse and a rider, when working together, is the most extraordinary combination of strength and intellect. That is precisely why horses and human beings are so complementary, why we make such a powerful team when working together.

When working with horses, as Chris Reeve learned, there also is danger. It is essential to be aware at every moment how strong and powerful they are. One slight mistake can prove fatal. When riding a horse you have to be living in the moment, too. You can't be thinking about a part you didn't get, what you want to do tomorrow, the fear of failure. You do that and you're done.

Admittedly, though, that ever-present danger is among those things that make riding so challenging and so rewarding. The first fear every rider has to face is falling off, and when it happens — because it will happen; everyone falls off at one point — you learn to deal with that fear and get right back on.

That day you get back in the saddle is the day you begin to become a rider.

The goal is to achieve a level of communication between the horse and the rider, which always seems to be just a little beyond reach. There is a language between the rider and the horse; at a certain level of expertise you are working together to achieve a common goal. It begins by establishing a hierarchy in which the horse understands that you are the alpha male and it must do what you say, as it would for the leader of the herd. Horses will question your ability to sustain that level of command, and you have to reinforce it firmly but not cruelly.

There is an expression popular in movies: A rider stays on the back of a bucking horse as long as necessary to "break" the horse. The meaning is to establish human dominance to the point at which the horse becomes almost docile. But the last thing anyone who loves horses wants to do is "break" one, rob it of its spirit. What you set out to do is channel that spirit into a compatible relationship. What I have been pursuing, with a passion, is a oneness between myself and my horse, a place at which we communicate with only subtle pressure. I have reached that place on certain occasions. I have hit it a couple of times, but it is a rare experience. It requires a perfection of balance, touch, experience, and total trust. It is as close to a *Star Trek* mind-meld as a human being and an animal might ever achieve. That feeling when we reached that point, when we were moving as one, is almost indescribable. And having experienced it, knowing it is possible, I want to feel it again, and again. So I continue to practice endlessly.

My passion for horses has changed my life in so many ways. More than thirty years ago, I was at the equestrian center in L.A. when I noticed a six-year-old girl whose mother had taken thalidomide while she was pregnant. This child, who had been born without hands and with only one leg, was sitting astride a horse. The horse was being led by two volunteers, one on either side so she wouldn't fall off. She was holding the reins in her toes and she had the most joyful smile on her face. It was such a beautiful sight that I started to weep. I asked, "What's going on?"

There was a charitable organization, it was explained to me, that funded therapeutic riding programs. I fell in love with this child and this charity. I could see the benefits of it in front of me. Horses, as I probably knew then but have since confirmed countless times, are amazingly sensitive animals with children and people in need. Some animals sense vulnerability and try to exploit it;

horses become gentle. It is an amazing trait.

I decided immediately to get involved in that charity. Since then the Hollywood Charity Horse Show, which has been sponsored for years by Priceline.com and Wells Fargo, has become another one of my passions. For the last three decades we have been running this show, raising between $300,000 and $500,000 every year for several charities. We've raised many, many millions of dollars. The event consists of a five-day horse show followed by a Saturday-evening party featuring such stars as Brad Paisley, Ben Folds, Lyle Lovett, Willie Nelson, Sheryl Crow, Randy Travis, Vince Gill, Wynonna Judd, and Neal McCoy, all of whom have volunteered their services. It has become one of the bigger horse shows of its kind in the country.

I've been fortunate to have assistants such as Kathleen Hays, who have done much of the heavy lifting in making this happen. The show is something my wife, Elizabeth, and I anticipate for months and from which we take great joy and satisfaction. The money we've helped raise has changed so many lives. Children who can't walk get to experience the freedom of movement. I saw a child whose parents believed would never talk suddenly start speaking. I've seen children who were deeply withdrawn suddenly come alive with their love for an animal. It has become a foundation of my life.

Our mutual passion for horses also brought Elizabeth and me together. Both of us lost our spouse, and just as I did, she found peace in horses. And eventually we found each other.

I also have a passion for motorcycles. I'm as comfortable on a bike as I am on a horse. I have spent a good portion of my life riding. When I was younger, I would go out into the desert on a motorcycle every Saturday when I was shooting *Star Trek.* There was a clause in my contract prohibiting me from riding motorcycles or piloting airplanes. I did both, knowing that if something went wrong that contract would be the least of my concerns. We would ride the hills and trails in the heat of the day, the cool of the night, and the darkness of the early morning. I have ridden through winter snowstorms and the summer desert heat. I often would get on my bike and ride up to Santa Barbara and back, more than three hundred miles, in a day. Once, while trailing the group with which I was riding, my bike hit a depression that might had been dug as much as a century earlier by a prospector searching for minerals. I took a bad fall. By the time I got my bike up, everybody else was long gone. The bike wouldn't start. I was stranded in the desert heat, dressed in leather and wearing a helmet. My choice was between leaving them on and suffering heat prostration and taking them off and being burned by the sun.

For a reason I will never understand I decided to walk with my bike out of the desert. I pushed the bike up and down hills, sweat rolling off my body. After a considerable period of time I saw a man on top of the next hill, waving his arms for me to come toward him. As I followed his instruction, I found a steep downhill road. I got on the bike and coasted down that road — right into a gas station. No one else had seen that man or knew who it might have been, so given my *Star Trek* background I decided my life had been saved by an alien.

That was my story and I stuck to it. It resulted in considerable publicity, never a bad thing for an actor playing the captain of a spaceship. But even that accident did not deter me from riding bikes.

Riding a motorcycle and riding a horse have one significant thing in common: both require complete focus. Either on a bike or on a horse, you are riding on the edge of disaster.

As I've gotten older, many people have suggested nicely that maybe I should think about cutting out riding. They try to find subtle ways to talk me out of it. It's very dangerous, they warn me. You might get hurt." "I know," I respond. "That's one reason I love doing it." I am driven by fear and anxiety from the moment I get on the bike to the moment I get off. Danger, fear, anxiety — these are among the primary sources of my passions. Without them, I would no longer be enjoying my life.

In the spring of 2013 I was at an autograph session in Downers Grove, Illinois, when a heavily bearded man who looked like he had just walked out of the Tennessee woods said to me, "I know you love motorcycles and we would like to build you a bike." The man wants to build me a bike, who am I to refuse? We spent twenty minutes talking. His name was Dylan Moller, he said, and he was the director of innovation for a company called American Wrench. American Wrench, I was to learn, designs and builds beautiful custom rides. He gave me his contact information. If it was a real offer, why wouldn't I accept it? In my life I've owned or ridden many different bikes, but no one had ever made an offer like this one.

Coincidently, a wonderful bronze sculptor named Douwe Blumberg, from whom I had bought several pieces, called and told me he had been thinking about sculpting a real motorcycle. He wanted it to be art deco, he explained, with leaping horses in front. He intended to build it on a Harley frame. "Douwe," I told him, "this is amazing. You're not going to believe this, but two weeks ago a guy told me he wanted to build a bike for me. Why don't I get the three of us together to talk about it?"

Douwe Blumberg and I met with Brian and Kevin Sirotek, the owners of American Wrench, in Lexington, Kentucky. We sat around a table discussing the design, and everybody began to get excited. This really was happening.

A few weeks later Douwe decided he preferred to work on his own project and withdrew. But the Sirotek brothers had become intrigued with the challenge of building an improbable motorcycle, an exotic bike unlike anything ever built. Well, sure, I was all for that.

They decided to build a motorcycle powered by a 500-horsepower Cadillac engine.

That sounded good to me. I could feel my

passions revving up: 500 horsepower! But as long as we were designing it, I told them I wanted it to be a three-wheeled covered bike, so it could be ridden in any weather. It also had to have a passenger seat as well as storage space for luggage and other supplies.

The design concept was incredible. It was named the Rivet. The brothers described it as a "Landjet." Their intent, they wrote, "is not only to draw attention to the pilot and the vehicle itself, but to showcase the art and craft of hand-built machines, done in the spirit of keeping America's 'routes' alive . . . [and] blow the minds of everyone who sees, pilots or experiences it."

I couldn't wait to get on that bike and ride. In fact, the concept was so exciting that I suggested, "I have a great idea. Let's ride the bike from Chicago to Los Angeles. It's twenty-four hundred miles. We'll take a week in the summer and really enjoy it. How bad can that be?"

They shared my enthusiasm. "We'll do it with you. We'll get some other people and really make an adventure out of it."

Okay. Great. And never one to miss an opportunity, I said let's enlist the American Legion and raise funds to help pay college tuition for the children of fallen heroes. The

American Legion was trying to raise $20 million. We certainly weren't going to raise anything near that, but we could raise many thousands of dollars and generate a tremendous amount of publicity for the fund. This concept began to grow, and then got bigger. Everything multiplied. It was like being on a show: We would climb to the top of the mountain and leap off. In reality, I wasn't going to climb to the top of any mountain, much less jump, but we were in the midst of our fantasy and we continued adding layer upon layer.

The plan was to take this amazing bike, which was now based on the design of the great B-17, halfway across the country accompanied by as many as thirty riders, including Vietnam and Afghanistan veterans. Along the way we would schedule events at American Legion posts in seven cities to raise thousands of dollars.

And then I broke the news to Elizabeth, who looked at me lovingly and said sweetly, "Are you out of your mind? You're eighty-four years old and you're going to drive a motorcycle through the desert in the summer?"

I could barely contain my enthusiasm. "And you're going to drive with me!" I said. "You'll ride on the back of the motorcycle!"

To which she replied, perhaps less sweetly, "I am not getting on the back of the motorcycle."

"Of course not," I agreed. "We're going to have a bus accompanying us. You can ride in the bus. It'll be great fun."

Liz and I had very different definitions of fun. But it didn't matter to me; my passion was now fully engaged. The plans were made; we laid out a whole schedule. It was going to be such a great event that it had to be recorded. I decided to make a documentary: *The Ride.* It was to be the amazing story of a group of determined men riding across America on beautiful bikes to raise money for the Legion's scholarship fund. I hired a film crew to come with us and a public relations agency to generate publicity. Every rider was given a GoPro, and we had three cameras and a camera truck. We had a bus for the production people and a mechanic in case the bike broke down. We packed food and drink for everyone. This was becoming a major production.

Finally, it was time to get started. I hadn't actually seen the bike, although I had seen illustrations of what it was going to look like. But I was continually assured it was beautiful and it was going to be ready to go on time. Five hundred horsepower!

Rrrrrmmmm! Rrrrmmmm! I could practically feel that power.

We did a week of publicity as we made our way to Chicago to pick up the bike and get started. We were scheduled to depart on Monday morning. Sunday night it started raining. Tornadoes hit the area. Tornadoes are considered a bad omen, but the weather forecast for Monday was promising. The storm was moving east and the day promised to be bright and clear. Unfortunately, our first scheduled stop was St. Louis. St. Louis was underwater.

It didn't matter. We were going to go. When you are living your passion there is no room for reality to get in the way. I was ready. The film crew was ready. Even Liz was ready. Only one thing was missing.

The bike.

I had rented a warehouse and set up the opening shot of my documentary. We were going to shoot it Sunday afternoon. This bike, my bike, this marvelous achievement of technological and artistic mastery, was going to be sitting by itself. The warehouse was going to be dark; two lights would be outlining this bike. I intended to dolly in slowly as the bike emerged from the darkness. I saw it in my mind; I had it all planned. I had the warehouse, the lights,

77

the cameras. The crew was ready; I was ready. The only thing that was missing was the bike.

The bike wasn't quite ready, I was told. But don't worry, this is the greatest bike ever built and it will be ready to roll Monday morning.

Okay, change of plans. There is nothing unusual about that on a film set. We rescheduled for Monday morning at six at the garage, which was located about ten miles outside Aurora, Illinois. That was a problem: I needed to get my opening shot before the media got there for a press conference at nine o'clock. It's going to be tight, I told myself, but I'm a professional. I can do this.

I went to the studio where the bike was being built at 5:00 A.M. This was the first time I had seen the bike. It was beautiful, a magnificent piece of machinery. But it didn't have a canopy. "What happens if it rains?" I asked. "We get wet," I was told. Okay! I agreed. I mean, look at that beautiful bike. Besides, I had often ridden bikes in the rain. There is nothing colder than your leather being soaking wet and going forty or fifty miles an hour on the freeway. After several miles hypothermia sets in. But I could do it if I had to. Maybe my passion was slipping a little bit.

There also was no passenger seat. "Don't worry," I was told, they would make a seat.

The list of things I had to remember not to worry about was getting longer. Then they started the engine, the 500-horsepower engine. The garage shook. It was amazing. Who cared about being wet. "It's almost ready," I was told. "Just a little more tuning up."

I walked out in front of the shop. Most of the work had been done by a father and son. The son, who was about twenty-five years old, was standing there. He looked at me and started crying. "Why are you crying?" I asked.

"Sir, I don't know," he said. "I keep crying."

"Are you happy it's finished?"

"Yeah," he agreed. I assumed those were tears of joy. Sometimes I make bad assumptions.

We had set up a large tent in front of American Wrench. We had invited the media to be there at nine. The response had been strong. It was a great story: I was this old guy and I was about to embark on the journey of a lifetime. I was going to drive twenty-four hundred miles on the greatest motorcycle ever built. We were going to raise thousands of dollars to send kids to college.

We were making a documentary that would raise even more money for the scholarship fund.

The bike was going to be concealed inside the tent. When the media was in place, we were going to open the tent for the big reveal. In my mind I could hear the oohs and ahhs as people saw this beautiful machine.

At 6:00 A.M. we were in front of American Wrench ready to shoot that beautiful image I had planned. All we needed was the bike. "They're leaving from the garage right now," Kevin told me. "They're on their way."

At seven Kevin told me, "There's been a slight delay. It won't be here till eight o'clock." I didn't panic. I never panic. We'll figure it out, I thought. I'll make it work.

At nine o'clock we had 150 people waiting in front of an empty tent. "Have something to eat," I suggested. "The bike is on the way." It finally arrived at eleven. They pushed it off the truck into the rear of the tent. I apologized to everyone for the delay; then we pulled back the tent flap and there it was: the Rivet!

And it was every bit as beautiful as promised, a futuristic vehicle somewhere between *Mad Max* and *Star Wars*.

I sat in the cockpit for the first time. It had an innovative steering system that required some getting used to. The various operating buttons had been identified with a marker. I found the starter and pressed the button: Wow! The power of that engine seemed to surge through me. I had never felt anything quite like it. I just absorbed it for a few seconds; it was every biker's fantasy coming true.

I was ready to drive it off the podium. I put it in gear — and it didn't move. The engine was roaring, and it continued roaring. That bike didn't move. Then, slowly, it started to roll down the ramp. Kevin was next to me screaming, "Stop, Bill! Stop the bike!"

My sense of drama took control and I let the bike roll several more feet before I pressed the brakes. I was sitting there in front of 150 reporters and cameramen, ready to embark on a twenty-four-hundred-mile journey on a bike that didn't work. I said, "Well, this is it till our next act!"

We went into an office to figure out what to do. Brian and Kevin were devastated. The American Legion representatives were devastated. I was devastated. What were we going to do? "I've made a fool of myself," I said. "I said I was going and now it doesn't go into gear or steer." Then I had an idea: "What happens if we rent a bike for me?" Someone else suggested, "We can ship the bike along." We figured out how to salvage the trip: We would rent a bike for me, truck the Rivet, and display it at every planned stop while trying to fix it.

We rented a three-wheeler from Harley. We put the Rivet in the back of a truck. Several people got into the bus. Liz got on the back of my bike — and we took off for St. Louis.

By the time we got to St. Louis, the floodwaters had receded and the sun was shining. It was a glorious day. Maybe I wasn't riding the greatest motorcycle ever built, but the feeling of being part of this event was still pretty amazing. We did the entire twenty-four hundred miles and helped the American Legion reach its monetary goal. There were some moments along the route when I was completely fulfilled. I was overwhelmed by the sensory details: the wind in my face, the scent of the road, the noise of the cars and trucks coming toward us. We went through cities and mountain passes, through endless miles of fields and then the desert. Several people suffered physical problems, but I did very well, except for fainting from the heat in a

Las Vegas motorcycle shop.

The bike never worked. At each stop we would wheel it off the truck and put it on display. In many ways it could have been a Douwe Blumberg sculpture — it was beautiful and it just sat there. People would walk around it admiring it. Then we would wheel it back onto the truck and drive it to the next stop.

The documentary remains to be edited.

But even with all of the problems, my passion for what we were doing never wavered. I was passionate about the challenges; I was passionate about the opportunity to spend a week on a motorcycle; I was passionate about raising money to pay for kids to go to college.

Mostly, though, I am passionate about continuing to be passionate. The pursuit of passions has influenced every aspect of my life. That has never wavered or changed: I am still in search of a perfect meatball!

What I have also learned, looking back on eight and a half decades, is that it is possible to sustain passion. Look at Sir Edmund Hillary, whose passion was climbing the highest mountain in the world. It had driven him until the day he finally reached the summit. And as he stood on top of the tallest mountain in the world, he might have looked around and wondered, Now what am I going to do?

He didn't. Instead he saw other peaks that needed to be climbed, mountains that offered different challenges to him.

Identifying and pursuing your passions is a beginning and, if you are as lucky as I have been, it has no end.

4.

AN EMOTIONAL APPEAL

The once-great attorney Denny Crane was talking to Shirley Schmidt, his lovely partner in the TV law firm Crane, Poole & Schmidt. In response to her question, he replied thoughtfully, "Judge Brown."

To which Shirley said, "Come again?"

Denny sighed, "I don't like it when you say that, Shirley. It puts pressure on me."

Denny Crane was the character I played in the TV series *Boston Legal.* Candice Bergen played Shirley Schmidt. What wonderful characters David E. Kelley created. But initially, at least, it was not a character I wanted to play. I had said yes to a variety of different projects that overflowed those blank pages. I told my agent I was too busy, I didn't have the time to do another series. I just didn't want to make that type of commitment.

But my agent persisted. "I know you don't want to do it. I don't want you to do it. But just go have lunch with David Kelley. I know the best Thai restaurant in the world."

Okay, maybe that part about the Thai restaurant isn't true, but the rest of it is. I made it clear that there was no way I was going to sign to do another series, but I agreed to have lunch. At that lunch, David Kelley told me about the character he had created for me. He described Denny Crane, once among the greatest attorneys in the nation, as someone who is slowly losing his connection to reality — but whose confidence and ego remain fully intact. But what I found most intriguing was that in his growing dementia Denny Crane had lost his inhibitions. He had direct contact with his emotions. Unlike most people, he was able to express and do whatever he was feeling.

That interested me. The ability to experience the full range of emotions, from ecstasy to grief, is the difference between a life lived in the shadows or in the brightest sunlight.

I agreed to do the series for one season. But I enjoyed playing Denny Crane so much that I stayed for our entire run.

Denny Crane didn't just experience his emotions; he broadcast them. He forced other people to deal with them, too. He was loud and bombastic and smart and lovable, but he lived life and he gave it no quarter. I have seen people shutting themselves off from real emotion. I've done it myself. No one wants to be in emotional pain. So they live life in the middle, never allowing themselves the free expression of emotion. It's certainly safer. But someone said to me once, the more you feel, the more you are capable of feeling. In other words, no one enjoys the pain of grief, of loss, but if you allow yourself to fully experience that, you are also opening yourself to fully experience happiness and joy and all the other emotions on the scale that eventually will follow.

All of us are born with access to an amazing tapestry of emotions, but for many people, somewhere early in our lives, we lose the ability to fully experience those emotions. The reasons for that are complicated, but the damage is real. One of the greatest horror films ever made was the original *Invasion of the Body Snatchers.* The monsters in this 1956 film were aliens able to produce duplicates of human beings identical to human beings in every way except one: They experienced no emotions. As one character explained it, "There's no emotion. None. Just the pretense of it. The words, the gesture, the tone of voice, everything else is the same, but not the feeling."

Becky, one of the townspeople who became aware of the threat, rails against it, saying, "I don't want to live in a world without love or grief or beauty; I'd rather die." But Becky falls asleep, allowing the aliens to substitute an emotion-free duplicate. This pod person looks and talks and acts exactly the same; in fact, her boyfriend, Dr. Miles J. Bennell, isn't aware of the substitution until, as he explains, "I've been afraid a lot of times in my life, but I didn't know the real meaning of fear until . . . until I had kissed Becky."

It's possible that an actor understands the emotional context of life more than any other professional. Portraying emotions is the actor's job. I have been asked many times if, as an actor, I actually feel the emotion of my character or if I just replicate the actions. In 1961 I starred in a Roger Corman movie titled *The Intruder.* I played an avowed racist who has come to a small Southern town to create a violent uprising against forced integration. It was a difficult story to tell at a very volatile time in our history, but worth telling, and we were filming in a small Southern town. This town did not want us there making a movie about racial issues. It was too close for them, too real. Their collective emotions were too exposed. The situation was so tense that when we first got there local law enforcement suggested we each plan an escape route to be used if the situation got out of hand. My plan consisted of going out the bathroom window of my motel room and racing into a cornfield.

The penultimate scene took place in front of the local courthouse, where I was trying to convince the townspeople to resist government meddling, to make the outsiders pay. I had a long speech that ended with me urging them to lynch the black leaders. It was an angry, vicious speech; I was spewing hatred.

Corman did not let local people read the script. That was a wise decision. But we needed a crowd for that scene, so we invited townspeople to be extras, offering food and fun. That scene was scheduled to be shot in the town square on Friday night. Fortunately, because we had a limited budget, we shot practically around the clock Monday through Thursday, and by Friday my voice was completely gone. The best I could manage was a whispered rasp. There was no way I could make that speech.

Roger Corman devised a solution. He shot the crowd over my shoulder as I said basically nothing, directing them when to cheer. He told these people, "Bill has lost his voice.

I'm asking him not to talk while we are shooting this scene." We spent four hours shooting it without the slightest problem. After the crowd had dissipated I managed to make that speech. By that time there were only a few people still there.

It was not an easy speech for me to make. My personal beliefs were the exact opposite of those of my character. Had I met him in real life I would have had nothing to do with him. And yet I had to say those words in a convincing manner. For those moments I had to feel that emotion. I had to put myself in the guise of a man who wanted to lynch another human being. And as I started saying those words I actually felt his hatred, his feeling of impotence as the world was passing by. It built inside me. As I made my speech I was filled with anger. I don't know where it came from, it certainly had nothing to do with this scene, but I was able to infuse the screenwriter's words with real anger and frustration.

One of those people who had stayed till the end was the editor of the local newspaper. Roger and I were walking through the square the following morning when he stopped us. "You guys are so smart," he said. Roger and I looked at each other; we knew that, but what had we done to bring it to his attention? About what? we wondered. Fifteen years earlier, he explained, a black man had been lynched in that square. He had been hanged from the tree we were using in the scene. Some of the people in the crowd had been there that night, and if they had heard my speech there is no telling what might have happened. By shooting the scene the way we did we had diffused any potential problems. That's why we were so smart.

For me, for those brief moments, the emotion, my anger, was genuine — but I never became that character. Yet the intensity of those moments lingered for a few days. You don't just walk away from those feelings. The emotion had physically roiled my body. It took me some time to come down from it, to come back to normal. Being able to display emotions was central to *Star Trek*. What made the character created by Leonard Nimoy, the Vulcan Mr. Spock, so unique was that his race had successfully suppressed emotions from their lives. In one of our shows, DeForest Kelley's Dr. McCoy explained the basis of humanity to Spock, telling him, "The release of emotions, Mr. Spock, is what keeps us healthy — emotionally healthy, that is."

To which Spock responded, "That may

be, Doctor; however, I have noted that the healthy release of emotion is frequently very unhealthy for those closest to you."

Several years later Leonard Nimoy and I spoke about working together on *Star Trek*. While we were filming, Leonard had remained distant, aloof. I said, "You were not exactly a fountain of fun on the set." He explained that he found it necessary to remain in character the entire day. That was surprising to me. "You spent twelve hours a day *being* Spock?"

He did. Leonard taught acting, so he knew what worked for him. The irony of that, of course, was that he spent all that time preparing to portray a character who suppressed emotions.

My work has forced me to understand the range of emotions, although many times I have been no different from anyone else in trying to keep my emotions in public in check. That's what we are taught. Other people don't want to have to respond to your emotional outbursts. So we learn that lesson and we repress those feelings, letting bits of them leak out when it's safe. But the reality is that the more you allow yourself access to your real emotions the richer your life will be. It took me a long time to understand and accept that.

Many of the actors I see today don't really express emotions; they imitate emotions. Please, don't think I am criticizing any actor. Not only wouldn't I do that, but I would be wrong if I did. The quality of work I see on television and in the movies these days is very good. But few of these people have been trained on the stage, and there is a difference. They have learned their craft in many instances by watching other actors portray emotions, and then they imitate that. So in some cases they actually are imitating an imitation of real emotion; they are that far removed from real feeling.

I was taught not to portray emotion but rather to create a full-bodied character and allow that character to experience the emotion. The truth is that at times I have been as surprised as anyone else by the reactions of my character. I have never tried to inject an appropriate emotion into a character. When my character reacts, I never think, I didn't know my character would do that; instead I might think, Whoa, isn't that an interesting aspect to that character. Unplanned unplanning.

There was a TV show in which I played a man whose grandchild has been found after being missing for several weeks. The writer was worried that I wouldn't know what to do. The director suggested a response. But I have felt the loss of children. I've felt that pain. As I began the scene I choked back sobs and used some of the author's words. But the emotion of that scene was real.

I hosted a TV interview show, which I called *Raw Nerve.* The title came from the fact that I wanted my guests to expose their real feelings. Sometimes I managed to make that happen, but equally often those lifelong layers of protection made it impossible for me to get to those real emotions.

I do remember the most inappropriate public display of emotion in my life. I was on the *Star Trek* set when my mother called to inform me that my father had died suddenly of a massive heart attack. I was devastated, devastated. Truly grief stricken. This man had been my foundation. I flew to Miami and arranged for his body to be shipped to Montreal. When we got to Montreal, I had to pick out his coffin. The funeral director took me into a showroom where the different coffins were lined up like TV sets. They ranged from a simple pine box to a lead-lined gold-embossed coffin. There were numerous variations of different quality, at different prices. I had to choose the box in which this man I loved so dearly would be buried.

As I was making this decision, I could not help but think about him. He had immigrated to Canada as a young boy. He had shined shoes and delivered newspapers and struggled to save enough money to bring his siblings to the Americas. His was a heroic story. He had become a successful manufacturer and salesman of inexpensive suits. He taught me how to fold a jacket, how to work hard, and how to save money. And as I stood in that showroom staring at these coffins I heard his voice telling me distinctly: "Spend the money on the living."

I bought him a nice pine box.

During his funeral the next day, that coffin was wheeled into the chapel. It was among the most difficult moments of my life. I was standing next to my sister Joy, and as our father was being eulogized I whispered to her, "Dad would have been very proud."

"Why?" she asked.

I said, "I got a great deal on the coffin."

"Why?" she asked again. "Is it used?" I couldn't help myself; I started laughing. I covered my mouth, but it was of little use. That so perfectly described our father. Of course Joy started laughing, too. Other people heard what we said and suddenly ripples of laughter moved like a wave through the chapel.

It was a glorious experience; that change of emotion from sadness to laughter made it memorable. It was the furthest thing from a lack of respect; it was, in fact, a celebration of his life in those few words.

After that service we went to the cemetery. The rabbi was a Cohen, a high priest, and for some reason he was not allowed to go to the burial. I remember thinking how odd that was, that a rabbi couldn't go to pray over dead people.

What I remember most about that day is the sound of the first shovelful of earth landing on the wooden coffin. That sound of permanent loss surged through my body. It was such an instant and overwhelming feeling of grief. By the time we left the cemetery that day it had subsided, but I have never forgotten it. A year later we returned to dedicate his headstone, and I have not been back there since.

Like just about everyone else, for much of my life I kept my emotions inside. But among the few real benefits of age is that you finally reach the point where you don't have to do that anymore. You realize, as I did, that it is not only okay but also healthy to be honest about your feelings.

In March 2017 my family gathered to

celebrate a birthday. During the night my beautiful fourteen-year-old granddaughter, a smart and wise young woman, asked me a very difficult question. Her grandmother, my first wife and the mother of our three children, was in a hospital suffering from dementia. "Papa," she said, "why can't you go see her?"

The entire table quieted. It was an uncomfortable moment. There were people sitting there who loved her and did not know or understand what had happened between us. I could have ignored the question or made some glib remark. That's what people generally do rather than avoid admitting to their emotions. Especially unpleasant emotions. Instead I said honestly, "Because I still have the rage."

And after a moment to consider that, she said to me, "I have the rage, too."

The truth is that I never got over being angry about our divorce and I couldn't pretend that I did. I know what I did to cause that divorce; I long ago accepted responsibility for my actions. So I explained, "I am still angry that I let her father, who had the money, force me to use all of my resources to buy the house that your mother and your two aunts lived in, in Beverly Hills, when I didn't have fifteen dollars in my pocket after *Star Trek*. I understood her anger, too, but it wasn't necessary to punish me like that for years."

Incredibly, as I said those words, I could feel the anger surging through me. All these years later, after so many people and experiences, that anger was still there. And it was still just as intense. It is amazing that after all these years it still had such a strong impact on me. All those years it was still inside me, still capable of moving me. That's the power of emotions to shape us.

We may think we have outgrown certain events, certain feelings, that they no longer have power over us. That's just not true, at least not for me. In fact, it reminded me of similar anger I had felt toward my mother, who offended me so often in so many ways for so long that our relationship colored every relationship I had with women for much of my life.

Calling Dr. Freud. Dr. Freud. Bill Shatner on line one for you.

There is a distinct advantage in suffering through overwhelming grief and desperate pain. My wife Nerine was an alcoholic. I was certain I could save her. I believed that my love for her, and her love for me for loving her unconditionally, would be stronger than her addiction. Leonard Nimoy, who understood addiction, who knew all about alcoholism, warned me that it was more powerful than I possibly could understand. I didn't listen. I married Nerine and eventually she drowned in our swimming pool. I found her floating there.

I've described the pain of that, but it's just words; there is no way to accurately convey that level of pain to anyone else. My grief was overwhelming. This was the type of pain that makes you think either I'm simply going to die or I'm going to kill myself. The intensity was so strong that for a time I told myself that rather than living with that pain, it is much better to feel nothing. It dwarfed all my other emotions.

For most of us, most of the time, our emotions are the background music of our life. I saw a demonstration once that I loved: It was a short film clip of a man walking across a room to answer the ringing phone. But each time the clip was played it was accompanied by different music. With the music the scene changed entirely: When it was light and jaunty we knew this was not a serious phone call; when it was deep and dramatic we knew that call might be life changing. In most of our lives the music is always playing in the background. We're happy, we're sad, we're bored, we're excited, but our emotions are subdued. The music is playing softly. And then, and then, the timpani thunder, the horn section begins blasting, and the emotion we are feeling takes complete control of our life. That was the grief I was feeling. The emotion was overwhelming. It took complete control of me both mentally and physically. My mind and my body were responding to it: I couldn't think of anything else other than my loss, and my body resonated with pain.

That is the power of emotion.

I didn't die and I didn't kill myself. In fact, eventually I was able to experience extraordinary happiness and joy. For me, I learned, grief hovered over me for a period of time. It was more than a year before that weight lifted from my heart. Then the cloud gradually begin to lift. I've never forgotten that pain, I can summon up an echo of it if I choose to, but eventually the beauty of life filtered in and the pain receded.

I carry that emotional memory with me: When I experience sadness or grief I draw on it. The pain is familiar, and I am reminded: Didn't I recover from this before? It provides the perspective that any emotion, every emotion, is temporary in nature and we will survive it.

Conversely, I have never forgotten the

emotional joys of childhood. Several years ago I was invited to participate in the biggest paintball fight ever conducted. Every child has played some version of good guys and bad guys; this was good guys versus the other team using guns that fired half-inch balls of paint. It was scheduled to take place in a 175-acre paintball facility in Joliet, Illinois, which has houses and forts and castles in which to hide, seek, and shoot. In other words, it was a big kid's fantasy come true.

Not only did I immediately accept, I also decided to film a documentary about it. The biggest paintball fight in history? I'm in. My wife, Elizabeth, immediately decided, "I don't want to get involved with this." It turned out she is a paintball sharpshooter, so she was in.

Five thousand people were participating. The rules are simple: If you got hit by a paintball, you had to sit out for fifteen minutes; then you got another life and could continue. I was appointed leader of one army. In a paintball war points are given for many different things. By far the most points are awarded for painting, for "killing," the leader of the opposition in their headquarters. Accomplishing that is worth almost enough points to win the entire event. But to prevent that, the leaders are very well guarded.

With that many players, lunchtimes are staggered. When our turn came, Liz and I were standing on line for a burger when the man standing behind me started weeping. We turned and asked if he was okay. "I'm so sorry, Bill," he said. The man had his paintball gun in his hand. Then he explained, "The head of the other team is a paintball manufacturer and he offered me a new gun if I snuck into your camp and assassinated you. But I like you so much I can't do it."

Being Bill Shatner pays off once again! "I have an idea," I said. We went through my strategy. I slipped several paintballs in my sleeve and said to him, "Point your gun at me. I'm your prisoner. Take me to the guy who sent you." We walked across the field into the enemy camp. As we got closer I saw their commander. When I was about twenty feet away I suddenly put my hands over my chest, screamed, "Oh, my God!" and fell down. I am an actor and I was portraying a heart attack victim.

Apparently my scene was believable. Their commander ran over to me and leaned down. At which time I smashed the paintballs on him. Then I did a Captain Kirk on him; I grabbed his pistol and pushed him down. "Don't move," I said, in my toughest tough-guy voice. We had captured the enemy commander.

The joy I was experiencing at that moment was no different than I had as a child seventy years earlier. I still had access to that emotion and I was able to experience it fully.

Another thing I have experienced in my life is the power of love to create emotions. By itself love isn't an emotion; instead it is a launching pad for emotions. Love is ecstasy, joy, happiness, comfort, sorrow, sadness, pain, and grief. It is thrilling, and it is chilling. It often is as difficult to live with it as it is to live without it. I sometimes think about the popular song "What I Did for Love." In my life the answer is simple: everything. Love is that thing so many of us spend great periods of our lives questing after, only to discover when we find it that it often doesn't live up to our expectations.

In my eighty-plus years I have experienced just about every type of love: I have enjoyed passionate, romantic, and unexpected love; I have found joy in parental love; it would literally be impossible to accurately describe the love I've had for my dogs and for my horses. I have loved certain characters whom I've played and casts that I've been fortunate enough to be part of! I have loved cars, motorcycles, food, and the occasional item of clothing. I love my house that I've lived in for more than four decades. I've loved singing and writing. I've loved being onstage and hearing the laughter and the applause from an audience. I've loved being part of an audience in the thrall of a great entertainer. I've loved the feeling of being alive. I've loved; oh, how I have loved.

And I've learned that each different type of love can create an entirely different emotional climate. Loving a relative or a child or a pet or a friend often is relatively easy and carries with it little emotional risk. Exposing yourself to loving another person carries with it tremendous risk.

The search for love can expose emotions that have been tucked away for a lifetime. We've all seen extremely successful and respected people suddenly lose control over their actions and end up destroying their reputations and sometimes their careers. A female astronaut puts on a diaper and drives halfway across the country to confront her lover. The chief judge of New York's Court of Appeals gets caught sending a condom and threatening messages to a woman who has ended their affair. In many cases these people have met someone who exposed them to new experiences, someone who has forced them out of their safety zone. Suddenly they are feeling things they have never felt before. Love can be addictive.

Several years ago I was working on a movie and the star was having an affair with his leading lady. That is not unusual. Nobody was concerned or even very interested in it. The problem was that he became so enamored with her that he came to the set unprepared day after day. He eventually turned the whole film over to her, and that became a problem for the rest of us. It was fascinating to watch this star being reduced to the proverbial "puddle of emotions." A few years later I saw our female star at an event. She had gotten married — to someone else. But she took the time to apologize to me, telling me how sorry she was for what had happened. "It got out of control," she told me.

Emotions run wild! Been there, done that. Early in my life it happened to me. Then it happened to me again. And again. I was a handsome man back then. I look at the photographs of myself at that early stage of my career and I think, Geez, I was good-looking. I didn't feel that way, though. Not at all. I had the looks, the physique, the desire, and the talent. I was one of those fortunate people to whom so much was given. Of course the compensation was that I didn't accept it. When I looked in the mirror I didn't like the reflection. I thought I wasn't especially attractive to women, and so I pursued them even more to make myself feel better. To complete myself. I didn't think much about love at that time, other than what the playwrights had written for my character or what the popular singers were telling me. What I knew mostly about it was that it felt good. At times it felt unbelievably good. But my definition of love was limited to a relationship between a man and a woman and what I was supposed to feel for my family.

That definition started changing when I was a teenager visiting New York City for the first time. I went to an afternoon movie by myself at the great Radio City Music Hall. A man sat down next to me. After a few minutes his hand drifted onto my knee. I had not the slightest concept of homosexuality at the time. I moved my leg, figuring I was taking too much space. But seconds later his hand was on my knee again. Then his hand was between my legs. I jumped up and screamed; I was terrified. I ran out of the theater, feeling violated.

What that stranger was expressing toward me was not love. Not at all.

But it was my first experience with a homosexual. I was at the beginning of my career in the theater, so obviously it would not be my last one. A year or so later I was stage-managing a show in Montreal. Our star was a French actor. He invited me to join him for dinner. I was thrilled, a fine actor asking me to have dinner with him. We were going to a nice restaurant, he said, and I needed a jacket. "Come up to my room. I have a jacket there to lend you."

Within minutes he was chasing me around the room. I tried to make a joke of it, but it gave me a glimpse of how someone in a subservient position might feel about being oppressed. I like to believe it changed my behavior toward women. I like to believe it. I do know it took me a while to understand that the same emotion I feel, and have identified as love, is exactly what everyone else feels, whatever their gender, whatever their sexual preference. I have a dear friend who is gay. Even as we became friends, and I knew he was gay, his sexuality was a subject we intentionally avoided discussing. Or at least I did. There was nothing to be said about it.

Then one day I saw a sadness in him and,

as a friend, asked what was wrong. A relationship had gone bad, he explained; he had been rejected. And what was so obvious was that the pain he was feeling was the same as I had felt when a relationship with a woman had turned out badly. We sat down and over time talked about love. I learned how ordinary, and at times tortured, love is for everyone.

What would the world be like without love? Well, for starters, there would be many fewer country songs. As many people might remember, I have explored a world without love in a series called . . . *Star Trek*! (The Applause sign is blinking!) My close Vulcan friend, Spock, grew up in a society that intentionally suppressed emotions because they are so powerful and potentially dangerous. Emotions, he had been taught, could be messy and troublesome, leading him to admit, "May I say that I have not thoroughly enjoyed serving with humans. I find their illogic and foolish emotions a constant irritant."

With the wisdom that comes from living eight decades on *this* planet I can write with confidence that Spock's Vulcan is not a planet on which I would ever choose to live. I wrote a song titled "Alive"; part of the lyric explains:

The day is alive with color and sound;
My joy is back and I'm glad I found it
Before it was too late.
The air carries the scent of hope and joy;
The breeze weaves its touch on my face
    and hair.
The scent of hope is in the air.

Many years ago, even before I was born, Sigmund Freud wrote: "Unexpressed emotions will never die. They are buried alive and will come forth in uglier ways." It isn't quite use 'em or lose 'em. Rather, it is use them or suffer the consequences. Emotions are the color and sound of our lives.

It is our emotions that can take us to heights and to depths of spirit that we can reach in no other way. What I've learned is to embrace them all, the pain as well as the joy, and let them resonate through my body. I can't tell anyone how to gain greater access to their emotions, but what I can write with confidence is that doing so will make a significant difference in your life, as it has in mine.

5.
THE BASIC INGREDIENTS: HEALTH AND (SOME) WEALTH

We Jews have traditionally described our culture through humor. Once, for example, an elderly Jewish man was crossing a street on New York's Upper West Side when a taxi came speeding around the corner and just clipped him, knocking him down. The people who saw it came running to help him. One man took off his own jacket, folded it, and gently slipped it under the victim's head. When the victim opened his eyes, the bystander asked him, "Are you comfortable?"

In barely a whisper the man replied with a verbal shrug, "I make a living."

"I make a living." That was my father. That was his ethic. More than anything, that might have been what I learned from him: Take care of your family. Work hard; earn a living; don't depend on anyone else. The historic slander about Jews has always concerned money; Jews were the money changers. That was always the foundation of the anti-Semitic slurs. The reality has always been very different, of course. The real foundation of Jewish culture has always been, as my father taught me by his example, work hard, take care of your family, give to others when you can. It isn't necessarily happiness that money buys; it is security.

Or, as great Jewish comedians have often reminded us, what is true for everyone, "Rich or poor, it's nice to have money."

I have been poor and I have been rich. I have lived both lives. I've lived in the back of a pickup truck and I've lived in a beautiful California home and on a Kentucky horse ranch. I know the real value of money. I know what it buys, but I also know what it costs. I have earned a considerable amount of money in my lifetime. Quite often people will come up to me and ask for financial advice. My response is immediate: laughter. I am the last person anyone should ask for financial advice. I tell them that if I knew what to do I would be doing it, I wouldn't be telling other people about it. I always wonder how people could fall for those so-called experts selling a course about how to become rich; doesn't it occur to people that if these "experts" really had that knowledge they would become rich by doing it, rather than preying on other people?

I have made my money by working, rather than investing. Many years ago the great Canadian actor Lorne Greene gave me an investment tip. "Buy uranium stocks," he told me. "It's going up!" Lorne Greene was a sophisticated investor, so I bought uranium. It was a can't-lose situation. The day after I bought it, the prime minister of Canada announced the country would no longer be mining uranium. I lost my entire investment. Through the years I have heard a lot of different advice about investing. Years ago my business manager, concerned that I was spending too much money on my horses, offered what he thought was sage advice: "Don't buy something that eats while you sleep." Another friend of mine who enjoyed gambling told me his secret of investing: "Never bet on anything that talks." So while I am not an expert, I have learned from many experts in different financial areas. And considering all the advice they have given me, I think I can sum up my strategy of investing: try to be lucky.

I think it is well known that I supposedly earned several hundred million dollars as the spokesperson for Priceline.com. What is much less known is the real story, which properly illustrates my financial acumen.

My late wife, Nerine, had a friend who had some connection to an internet start-up site named Priceline.com. It was an interesting concept; rather than setting a price on things or services like an airline ticket or a hotel room, buyers named the price they were willing to pay and Priceline.com tried to find a supplier of that product or service who would accept that offer. Like any start-up, they had limited resources, so Nerine's friend asked me if I would do a radio commercial for them.

Here's the best business advice I can give: When the phone rings, say yes. Don't even say hello; say yes. I told them I was going to New Zealand and would do it there. I knew nothing about the company; I did it because the people seemed nice and my wife asked me to do it.

That commercial was successful, so they asked me to do several more. Unfortunately, they said, they couldn't pay me in dollars, but they would pay me in stock. I knew about the internet boom. So I agreed.

Eventually I owned quite a large number of shares, which originally were valued at about $0.25 each. And then the company caught fire. I helped, I know I helped, bring attention to them; the commercials were well written, but it also was a good service.

It helped people save a lot of money. The value of the stock kept rising. I would look at the paper every day and I couldn't believe it. In that paper I was a wealthy man. The stock went from essentially no value to about $175 a share. Suddenly I was worth a lot of money. By that I mean I was worth enough money to spread it to those in need and still have a significant amount left over. I would read stories about how wealthy I had become: Supposedly I was worth several hundred million dollars.

Let me repeat that: I was worth several hundred million dollars. (Please note, this time I left out the "supposedly.")

I knew very little about being worth several hundred million dollars in the newspaper. It had never happened to me before. Obviously. But then I learned about something called a lock-up. This is a law that prevents people from selling stock for a period of time. It was passed to prevent people from starting a company, running up the value of the stock, then selling, leaving shareholders with a worthless company. My lock-up prevented me from selling my stock.

While I was waiting, the dot-com stock bubble burst. The value of my stock plummeted. Many dot-com companies went out of business, but Priceline.com managed to hold on. Eventually I sold my stock for considerably less than it had been worth. Let me put it this way: It had once again become a penny stock.

After I sold it the value started rising again, because it is a good company. The value went up to more than $1,000 a share. So as it turned out I made my usual mistake: I held it when I should have sold it; I sold it when I should have held it. It was an interesting learning experience and the next time I'm worth several hundred million dollars on paper I won't make the same mistake.

Which is why no one should ever ask me for financial advice.

In fact, for most of my life I have had considerably less money than publicly believed. People looked at the tremendous success of the *Star Trek* series and assumed the cast had continued to participate financially in that phenomenon. The economics of Hollywood can be summed up succinctly: The other guy gets most of the money. It doesn't even matter who the other guy is; somehow the contract benefits him. With the *Star Trek* series, for example, for many years while the studio was making millions of dollars we got nothing. We earned no residuals, no bonuses, no nothing. We had to take legal action to get even a small part of the earnings. In fact, it was only much later in my career, when my name had value attached to it, that I began being paid considerable sums of money.

I have earned a substantial amount of money in my career. It is still kind of shocking to me that the same person who once skipped breakfast so he could afford to go to the movies in the evening has become financially secure.

There are many things that will make a significant difference in your life, but all of them begin with health, love, and wealth. They are the dominant factors in most people's lives. They determine pretty much everything else. Which of course reminds me of another aphorism I remember hearing as I grew up: If you have your health, you have everything. Although what could it hurt if you also had a nice house?

When I was growing up our health was not a topic of much concern; we were expected to be healthy. In those days there didn't seem to be much you could do about your health. The Mediterranean diet? The Paleo diet? Our diet was a lot simpler: You ate what was in front of you if you knew what was good for you. It was only many years later, when I could afford to go to the best doctors, the physicians who had these amazingly sensitive machines, that I could afford to find out that I had cancer. If I hadn't been so successful Liz and I wouldn't have even known we had these cancer cells in our body.

Money is important. I wish I could say idealistically that money is not important, love is important, but money is the modern-world version of going out from the camp-fire and killing the protein so your woman and children can eat. It is that basic. It takes the form of currency, but when you leave the cave in the morning you really are going out to slay the beast. You are going to get the groceries.

Money has a direct relationship to survival. And as you go through life you become responsible for the survival of other people, so you need even more money to take care of that.

I learned that lesson from my father. His beast turned out to be inexpensive men's suits. People often talk about the sweet smell of success. In my life it wasn't a smell; it was the loud sound of some success. My father was a clothing salesman and later became a manufacturer of inexpensive men's suits. He was Montreal's Willy Loman, a very hardworking man who spent many years worrying about next month's bills. Montreal at that time was not an especially wealthy city, and there was a market for nice, cheap men's clothing. He had a small operation, three or four people in a fifty-by-fifty-foot room cutting and sewing. I remember the sound far more than the smell: the sound of the blades, the pressers, the rat-tat-tat of the sewing machines; that was more than half a century ago and I still hear it. There was a secretary in the front office who took orders: "I want twenty garments, sizes thirty-four to forty."

My father was the sales force. He would travel to different cities selling his suits. At times he would be gone for the whole week. He would come home exhausted on Friday night. Eventually his business became more successful, and the name became Admiration Clothing. Economically, we were "comfortable." We were lower-middle-class people. My dad did a good job keeping my mother and their three kids afloat. I had a bicycle, but I always had to work. I don't actually know if my father had ever had dreams that had to be set aside to support his family.

Because of my father, I could afford to have a dream. And my dream was to become an actor. Money was never a motivating factor for me. Which was necessary, because after all these years I have yet to meet a single person who went into acting for the money. Unlike in the garment business, nobody needs to buy a new actor to wear every couple of years. It is a profession in which you live from job to job and you never know if the phone is going to ring again. I started acting on radio when I was six years old, so I have been doing this for eight decades. According to IMDb, I have appeared in 238 movies or series or programs, I have appeared as myself in 393 programs, I have directed thirteen movies or TV shows, written eighteen, and produced twenty-two. I have done video games, soundtracks, five albums, almost fifty books, and even done virtual reality. I have earned and saved enough money that making a living will never be an issue for me. And yet I am as much in pursuit of the next project as I was half a century ago. I still feel that anxiety when the phone doesn't ring and I begin to wonder, What if my career is over? What'll I do?

My father certainly tried to talk me out of acting as a career. Find a job that gives you security, he told me. The paycheck makes the difference. Actors don't get regular paychecks. An actor lives from job to job. Many people have heard the expression "make your nut," which means to earn enough money to pay your expenses. The derivation of that expression comes from the theater; it's not something a playwright wrote; it's the way actors were thought of. In the American West, actors would travel from town to town by wagon, setting up their show for a week. It was exactly like a traveling circus, although lacking the appeal of the exotic animals. Usually, when the acting troupe arrived in town the local law enforcement officer would literally take the lug nut from the wagon wheel and hold on to it. Only after he had confirmed that the troupe had paid all its bills, to the hotel, to the inns, would he return the nut. Paying your bills thus became known as "making the nut."

The majority of actors never earn the nut. It's a profession with an enormously high failure rate. It is not a profession anyone goes into for the money. But when my father realized I was determined to do this he supported me — emotionally. He didn't have any money to loan me. He did help me buy a car for $400, and that required a sacrifice for him. And he encouraged me, which did have tremendous value.

Like every young actor, I struggled. I blundered on and wandered from one job to the next, sometimes half-starving, sometimes not going to the laundry, often not going to the movies, but I was very proud of the fact that I always paid my rent, I never stood in line for an unemployment check (to which I was often entitled), and I never asked anyone for anything.

My goal, my dream, was to have $1,800 in the bank. I don't know where that number came from, but it represented success. If only I could save $1,800! Eventually I did; I could look at my bankbook and see it: $1,800! I was living in New York, I was married and had children, but I was never able to save more than that. Our car would break, something would happen to a pipe, and our savings would go down to $1,000.

I lived with an element of fear all the time. How am I going to pay the rent and feed my family? *Star Trek* enabled me to get ahead for the first time. I was rich; I had $2,100 in the bank! And then my wife decided to divorce me. There went my $2,100 — and a lot more. That divorce cost me everything. When *Star Trek* was canceled, I was Captain Kirk, I was a legitimate TV star, and I couldn't cash a $15 check. I used my last few dollars to put new tires on my truck and put a camper in the rear bed, so I could get from summer theater to summer theater and have a place to live. That fear of being broke never went away. I've lived with it the rest of my life.

There are many people who believe that money plays a much too important role in people's lives. Mostly, I've found, the people who believe that have enough money so that they don't have to worry about it. But I have learned a few things about money: First, the obvious, it is better to have money than not have it. Money makes life easier, although conversely the pursuit of money often makes life more difficult. Second, live within your means; and third, try to stay out of debt.

And fourth, many people too easily equate money and happiness. I have known a lot of wealthy people, and while some of them were quite happy, many others were not. They had made their fortune believing money was the key to their happiness and discovered when they got it that they were no happier than they had been earlier in their life. So their quest to make even more money continued, with them believing more money might make them happy. In some instances, it will. Conversely, I have known many people who have struggled or are securely ensconced in the middle class who are very happy. They have built a life for themselves within the bounds of their earnings capacity that brings them joy.

Money is neutral. It has been said that the only thing money can't buy you is poverty. But it doesn't buy happiness either. It simply can make happiness possible.

I have always been careful with money. I inherited my economic philosophy from my father: Buy wooden coffins. My strategy was simple: Keep that monthly nut as low as possible. I would buy things I needed with the money that I had managed to save. That way I would own those things without having to make payments. For that reason I never leased a car or took a loan to buy a car; I bought a car I could afford at the time, often a used car. When I bought a home, I paid for it without taking a mortgage; that way I wouldn't have to worry about how to make the monthly payments.

More than anything I own, that house represents my security. I have lived there for more than four decades; I have experienced the best and the very worst of life in that house. And there has never been a moment when I thought about moving.

I'm no different from anybody else. I like shiny objects. I like men's toys. But things make almost no difference in my life. I can now afford to drive wonderful cars and I do, and I enjoy it, but I would do fine without those cars. I own horses and I love them, but if I didn't own horses I'd be at a riding stable renting a horse by the hour. I am not an ostentatious person. Long ago I realized that the things that really matter in my life aren't dependent on money: My wife, Liz, and my daughters and their families. My dogs. Riding horses. Having people whose company I enjoy over to the house to watch *Monday Night Football.* Discovering new hole-in-the-wall restaurants. The luxury to be creative and continue acting and writing and producing. The opportunity to travel and have adventures. My health, obviously. And my house.

The place with the light in the window. When I finally began working regularly on television I bought a house in Beverly Hills. It wasn't for me; it was a place for my kids to live with their mother. It wasn't in the finest part of Beverly Hills, but it allowed them to go to the Beverly Hills schools, which are wonderful.

I was living in a small cottage in Studio City. Every day I would run a three-quarter-mile loop through the hills, and when I did I would see this lovely house on top of a hill. And I would dream that one day I would be successful enough to own that house. One day I finally walked up that driveway and asked, "Is this house for sale?"

"You know," the owner said, "it's the damnedest thing. I just put it up for sale."

I raced down to the Realtor's office and got in line. I was able to buy the house for $100,000. I have lived in that house ever since.

The house has changed as I have. I have rebuilt it almost completely three different times. My neighbors have moved in; their families grew up and then moved out. I stayed. It might have been less expensive to move, but that was never a consideration for me. It is familiar to me. It is comfortable. This has been the house with the light in the window. You can look out from this house and see the sunrise and the sunset. It was the house in which Nerine died, after which we did an Indian ceremony so her spirit might rest. I buried two dogs under our fruit trees. That house is my adult history. Why would I want to be anywhere else? Because a new house has bigger bedrooms?

The memory of my early struggles still dominates my life. I know I am financially secure; I just don't feel that way. My feelings about money, I have learned, aren't necessarily rational. Which, ironically, probably puts me in the majority. The fear of being in debt has plagued me my entire adult life and I expect at this point it will never go away. To me, it's like having an emotional junk drawer, a place in which you just throw all the odds and ends and in the back of your mind you know that someday, when you get a little extra time, you're going to clean it out. Well, I have come to accept the fact that I am going to die with my junk drawer in disarray. Other people are going to have to go through it and wonder, What the heck is this and why did Bill save it? But I have also come to accept I am never going to be free of my fear of financial failure. Instead, I have learned to live with it.

I still don't spend a lot of money on myself. I am completely comfortable with my life. I don't need bigger and better and brighter to change my life. I don't want to change my life. I am encouraged all the time by everybody to spend more money on myself. "Have a good time," they say. And in response I tell them that I am having the greatest time. I am doing the things that make me happy with the people who make me happy.

When I was considerably younger, like

many people, I wondered what I would be doing differently with my life if I suddenly had financial security. The answer, I told myself, was pretty much "nothing." I loved what I was doing and couldn't imagine I would be happier doing something else. And then, as the years passed, I earned that financial security. I could afford to do pretty much anything I wanted to do, or even do nothing. It turned out I was right; I simply continued doing exactly the same things I had always been doing. Although admittedly I did so in a better car. And I slept better at night.

It is said you can't buy health, but money can at least help maintain good health. Good health is not an accident. It is a subject you can educate yourself about. The knowledge is there for you. I have had good fortune: I didn't step on an exposed electrical wire. I avoided being hit by a car. And I had the good sense to be born to parents with good genes. I have been given the gift of good health by my parents and their parents. I have my own philosophy about that. Throughout history the Jews have been an oppressed people. In ancient history they were slaves. The Jews who survived had to be smart and physically fit. And they handed those traits down genetically through the ages. Now, I don't know if that is actually true or not, but it makes sense to me.

But that gift of good health has made everything else possible: Without it, life can be a struggle. Just getting out of bed can be the greatest effort of your day. You have no room for love or anything else; you simply live in survival mode.

Having access to good doctors and medical care obviously is important, but it isn't enough. Good health is the result of what you do every day, as well as your luck in the gene pool. For a long time I have paid attention to what medical science told me were the best ways to maintain good health. I read the books and magazines and incorporated that information into my daily life. And when they announced that everything they had been recommending was wrong and changed it completely, I continued to follow their advice.

In addition to genetic engineering, I have learned that maintaining good health also requires you to be aware of the importance of diet, exercise, and, by association, your mental attitude. When someone tells me they are coming down with a cold, I always tell them that I don't get colds, I don't get sick. If I do get sick I forget about it quickly; the way I describe it is that I don't get sick until I am reminded that I am sick.

I believe that the foundation of good health is your mind-body connection. We do know that people who think they heal faster do heal faster. It is vitally important to tap into that and unleash the power of the mind to protect and heal your body.

Complicating the problem of knowing what's good for you is the reality that achieving and maintaining good health has substantial value, in particular to people selling that vast universe of products that supposedly keep us healthy. The general rule I tend to follow is that if it sounds too good to be true then it probably isn't true. Vitamins and supplements, for example, are a multibillion-dollar market. But the reality is that there is very little compelling evidence that most of these products have any real value. Except to those people selling them. Most people get all the vitamins they need from their diet. The exception seems to be vitamin D, which isn't actually a vitamin but rather is a hormone. Nobody really knows what it does, but there seems to be some evidence that a deficiency of vitamin D is associated with several serious diseases and conditions. Most people who live in the West or the South get sufficient vitamin D from sunlight, but those people living north of the Mason-Dixon Line, especially in the Northwest and Midwest, can't get enough of it naturally much of the year and should be taking a supplement. But as for other vitamins and supplements I have always believed that if it makes you feel better to take them, then it is worth the cost.

I have never been pillaged by false claims. I am skeptical enough that I have never been taken in by someone who is going to make me rich overnight or healthy. But I probably barely avoided it. My active curiosity has led me to seek out information. I have some knowledge of Chinese pharmacology and India's Ayurvedic medicine and I subscribe to trying them. I do try things; when I read that beets will lower your blood pressure within twenty minutes after eating them, I ate some beets. Why not? As far as I know, no one has died of an overdose of beets! I understand it all might be snake oil, we certainly are offered enough of it, but my curiosity compels me to at least try these things.

The truth is we all want to know what's good for us. Every few years some fad diet or exercise craze comes along that supposedly makes a difference. Now we are in the midst of the organic revolution. Organic foods are supposed to be very healthy for us. Maybe they are. But there is little real science to support that.

When I was growing up we knew nothing about healthy living. My father strived for one thing, to keep his family whole and well: At that time that meant meat on the table at night and cake or some other sweets for dessert. We didn't know that sugar could be bad for you. We knew nothing about the benefits of eating vegetables and fruits. We weren't even aware that smoking was killing us. We had no idea how to take care of ourselves. I remember sitting in a movie theater watching the incredibly dashing Paul Henreid put two cigarettes in his mouth, light them both, then take one out and hand it to his glamorous lady and they both puffed contently. Smoking was considered romantic and loving. Who knew?

And gradually health was transformed from a desire to an industry. The government began telling us what was good and bad for us. They created the food pyramid, illustrating what we should be eating. I paid attention to all of it. Several years ago I was on my way to dinner with Dr. Mehmet Oz and a cardiologist friend of his. On the way to the restaurant I read an article in the *New York Times* announcing that the food pyramid was wrong; instead of eating a lot of carbs and little meat and fat, we should be eating more meat and fat and fewer carbs.

At dinner I asked them how they could explain this complete reversal. I said there must have been evidence in their journals that justified this announcement. They sat there with a shamed look on their faces, like teenage boys caught making out with the neighbor's daughter. In fact, they had no explanation. They had been fed the same knowledge that we got.

So what we believe we know is evolving. But there are several things that we know for certain that make a difference. These things are settled; they are not going to change. The first thing I did for my health was stop smoking. I smoked: I wanted to be as sophisticated as Paul Henreid; I wanted to light two cigarettes and casually hand one of them to Bette Davis, who would puff on it enticingly until the moment of romance struck!

And then the surgeon general issued a report in 1964 stating flatly that smoking was deadly. That certainly was a strong way to spoil the romance. I stopped smoking about three years later: We were shooting *Star Trek* and four of us were in a limo on the way to a promotional appearance. We started talking about the surgeon general's report and each of us in turn said why we were willing to give up smoking. One person said he would do it to prove he had the discipline. When my turn came, I said I would do it because my daughters were refusing to kiss me, making faces, and telling me I smelled like cigarettes. We opened a window and in unison threw out our packs. (Littering wasn't such a big deal then either.) I never smoked another cigarette. I was fortunate; for whatever reason it was not an especially difficult thing for me to do once I'd made the commitment.

Unfortunately, Leonard Nimoy could not stop and eventually it did kill him. After he was diagnosed with chronic obstructive pulmonary disease, a lung disease caused by smoking, he asked me several times, "Bill, why didn't you make me give up smoking?" No one can "make" another person give up an addiction. All we can do is cite facts: Smoking kills. There is no doubt about that. But it also causes several other chronic diseases that make life more difficult. So at the top of the list of things to do for your health is stopping smoking.

Next is exercise. Smoking will shorten your life; exercise will lengthen it. I have always been active and I remain so. While

I've never spent too much time in gyms, I have always found ways of exercising. I am fortunate enough to have a heated pool and I run in it; many people swim, but I can only swim ten or so laps, so instead I run like hell in the water for about thirty minutes. I try to do it pretty much every day when I'm home. It is difficult, but if the great flood ever comes I will be able to run through it!

But I do substantially more than that. I am eighty-seven and I'm still lifting two twenty-five-pound weights several times a day. I used to run; now I walk as much as I can — which isn't much, due to my surgery. But my greatest exercise is riding. Anyone who believes riding a horse is not exercise has never ridden a horse. It requires movement, muscle strength, and endurance. If you are not in decent condition riding will wear you out, tax your muscles, and result in considerable discomfort. When I'm in L.A. I ride as often as I can. I'll ride several times a week if possible.

As for my diet, I have been given the gift of Elizabeth Shatner, who has taken a real interest in healthy eating. I am an experienced eater; I have been doing it successfully for more than eight decades. But I have tried to change my diet, even knowing how flimsy the real data is. I don't officially refer to myself as a vegetarian, but I don't eat nearly as much meat as I once did. I'm not sure it makes any difference, but it makes me feel good, so I do it. I also have learned to stay away from bread because the carbs in bread turn immediately to sugar, which can be a cause of diabetes. Elizabeth and I are not picky eaters; we're careful eaters. She does the best she can for us with salads and vegetables and non-bread grains. Years ago, if I had been told I would be extolling the taste of crispy beets, I probably would have doubted you. But Liz slices them, puts them in a pan with olive oil, and heats them until they are crisp. They are delicious, and you can put anything on them.

Is that healthy? I believe it is; therefore it is. Nothing is more important to maintaining good health than your mental attitude. Some people believe meditation makes a significant difference in their health; if they believe it, it does. We think we know so much, but we know so little. We don't have the slightest real knowledge how important a positive mental outlook is to maintaining good health. We do have some evidence that laughter actually makes a difference in the state of your health, and we know that placebos can be effective, sometimes even more effective than the drugs they are being tested against. There is no scientific reason that should be true, except that the person being given the placebo believes it will help.

I know people who only get sick when they have finished their projects. They are able to keep the demons away while they have work that has to be done. But when they allow themselves to relax, they give themselves permission to be sick.

I never talk about how I'm feeling. I listen to other people talk about their physical problems, and I hear them trying to top each other: "I've got to have my knee replaced." Okay, I'll meet your knee and raise you a hip. Nobody wants to hear about another person's problems. If someone asks me how I'm feeling my answer is always the same: "Terrific." "I feel so good there could be two of me." I say that no matter how I am feeling. I am of the opinion that you can seduce yourself into thinking you are healthier than you are. If you get a cold and are not contagious, staying in bed isn't helpful. All you can do is lie there moaning about how bad you are feeling. If you can get up, get up, go outside, move around. I'm not talking about a serious disease; that's a whole different situation. But for many minor problems I believe you can talk yourself into feeling better than you actually do.

Finally, get enough sleep. Sleep is always difficult for an actor. When you're working you are often so busy learning lines, rehearsing, developing your character, that there isn't time to get sufficient sleep. If you're working in the theater you're usually so charged up after a performance that you can't go to sleep. And when you aren't working then the fear that "maybe this is it, maybe my career is over" takes charge and if you can manage to overcome the anxiety and get to sleep it's generally restless.

It isn't only actors who struggle to get enough sleep. Most people do. Years ago I had a conversation with a physician, who told me there was only one cure for insomnia: "Get plenty of sleep."

Ironically, I have spent my life dreaming about getting more sleep. Usually without success. There always seems to be just a little more to get done than time to do it. But sleep is vital for good health. Your body needs that time to replenish and heal. The experts recommend adults should get between seven and a half and eight hours' sleep a night. That is a vital ingredient in good health. I know people who worry so much about not getting enough sleep that it keeps them awake for hours.

Here's what I've learned: There are steps we all can be taking to maintain our health. There are no secret formulas or magic potions. Balance matters: Don't smoke. Stay active. Eat sensibly. Remind yourself how good you feel. And get as much sleep as you need. For me, at least, so far, so good.

6.
MY CURIOUS QUEST FOR ADVENTURE

Throughout my adult life, in an effort to understand more about who I am and what is this wonderful gift we have been given, I have on occasion found myself coming back to a few profound questions, among them: What the hell am I doing here? How did I get into this? And perhaps most important, How am I going to get out of this?

I don't think of myself as an adventurer. Meaning I don't set out to put myself in precarious situations. I'm probably not someone who would have gotten into a ninety-foot-long sailing vessel and sailed into the unknown, believing there were demons just below the surface. I don't necessarily equate being adventurous, taking a chance, with being a test of courage. Rather, I am someone who tries to satisfy my curiosity. Which is why I have often ended up in precarious situations.

With age comes the expectation that you

have acquired wisdom. Sages and gurus are never depicted as young men or women. They are most often wizened old men who pontificate in sometimes mysterious words. They are the people sitting on mountaintops or in remote places who supposedly have discovered the secret of life — and are willing to share it with people searching for . . . the answer. While in my acting career I have had many encounters with these people, I've only played one once. In the sitcom *Third Rock from the Sun,* I created the character of the Big Giant Head. Big Giant Head was the commander of the four aliens living on Earth disguised as human beings. And he wasn't written as an especially wise man. In fact, when he was challenged his response was simply, "The yelling will cease and the killing will commence!"

Because I have lived more than eight decades, people have mistakenly assumed I have acquired that knowledge and so I have been asked that question: What is the secret of life?

Here's the answer: If I knew, it no longer would be a secret. I would shout as loud as I could for everyone to hear: "Here it is! Here's the secret of life!" For me, the answer has been simple: Keep living. I have always been open to new experiences. More than anything else, my philosophy of life has been: Say yes, yes to life. That isn't a secret.

I don't know where this need to abandon security and seek adventure comes from. I actually should have been exactly the opposite: I have this terrible fear about being alone and yet throughout my life I have left loving arms and gone out into the world without knowing where I was going. It sometimes is incomprehensible to me that a person who so craves the warmth of familiar places would try to become an actor. Acting may well be the least secure of all professions. There is no such thing as security; there is only "I hope I get another job." In other professions you follow a well-trod path; you go to school, you learn your trade, you take whatever professional courses are necessary, and you become a doctor or a lawyer or an appliance repairman or a plumber or a teacher. Why would an insecure person like me become an actor?

Dr. Phil, calling Dr. Phil.

The only thing that makes sense to me is that I have a need for adventure. I have to continually keep challenging myself. I need that thrill. I started out on this path with nothing; no money, no contacts, no real prospects. It was both terribly frightening and unbelievably thrilling. When I left Montreal, I went to those strange cities of Toronto and Ottawa. I didn't have a home; I had no friends there; I had no acquaintances. I lived in the least expensive places I could find. As bad as it was, I knew I was in the midst of an adventure. I didn't know what was going to happen the next day. I didn't live with the hope that the phone was going to ring suddenly and change my life, because I didn't have a phone. I remember, I literally can summon up the memory of lying on a rope mattress in an attic room, a five-flight walk-up, being so lonely I wanted to cry, knowing I was sharing that space with mice, and somehow being okay with it. I knew intrinsically I was in the middle of my great adventure. Whatever was going to happen, I found great comfort in the reality that I was not going to live my father's life. I have never lost the feeling that something interesting and fascinating and maybe thrilling is waiting for me just ahead, if I have the courage to be open to it.

Scientists now have evidence that new experiences build new brain cells. The logic is unassailable: Active people stay involved in life longer than sedentary people. I have been able to sustain my sense of adventure. So I get on a motorcycle, I ride a horse, I travel to strange places, I continue trying to explore and expand my horizons.

Now, truthfully, I have never intentionally set out to risk my life — that just happened. But the exhilaration of being in a life-threatening situation, that feeling of total immersion in life, is overwhelming and unforgettable. Especially when I am safely back on the ground.

It is those experiences that make life so worth living. For example, I have long enjoyed paramotoring. Essentially, this is our version of Icarus: It involves simply a small motor attached to a large kite. I learned how to do it on the beaches of Ventura, where there generally are sufficient winds. I literally would fly with the birds. It is a wondrous experience, made even more exciting by the fact that it can be dangerous. We all have seen power mowers fail; this is essentially a power mower. But when you are in the air you are totally in control; you are the master of your fate.

I have an array of normal fears in my life, and among them is a fear of heights. Maybe it is because of the man I saw standing on the wing when . . . oh, wait, that was *The Twilight Zone.* It is ironic, though, that even though I became best known as a Starfleet captain, heights have always made me uncomfortable. But I haven't allowed that fear to stop me. When I had the opportunity to try paramotoring I did and loved it immediately. I found myself a hundred feet in the air, looking down on the beach, bouncing along the rising thermals as if they were invisible waves. The only sound was the dull chugging of the engine behind me. I took advantage of every opportunity to fly.

So when I was asked to participate in the historic paintball war I had a great idea to generate publicity: I would paramotor to the site. Yeah! Yeah! Everybody thought it was a great idea. A paramotoring club made plans to fly with me.

It was approximately three miles from the takeoff point to the designated landing site, but the route took us over the Ohio River. I was a little concerned about it; I didn't know anything about the landing site. For all I knew there might be large rocks there that had to be avoided. I also knew nothing about the prevailing winds. I was experienced, but I certainly wasn't an expert. The club members assured me it was quite safe: "We mapped it out." At least no one said those four fateful words: "What could go wrong?"

The day was warm and beautiful. I put on my five-point harness, grasped the controls, and took off. You control this device with a dead-man's throttle, which is similar to riding a motorcycle. When you hold tight, gas flows into the engine keeping you aloft; when you cut back on gas flow, the propeller slows and you begin to fall slowly. If you let go entirely, the engine will stop. While you're pressing this throttle you also are holding on to the kite, which you can guide left, right, up, or down. So I was holding two controls in my right hand, both of which will keep me in the air or cause me to fall.

We took off and for the first few minutes the flight was perfect. I followed several men over a beautiful landscape. And then in the distance I saw we were approaching the Ohio River. The very broad Ohio River. The really wide Ohio River. As we reached the river I saw the electrical power lines along its banks. It occurred to me that this was a dangerous situation. If I should get caught in a wind gust it could take me right into those electrical wires. I could feel the palm of my right hand beginning to sweat.

Well, that wasn't helpful. My hand began slipping. By the time I crossed over the wires I was really sweating. I was over the river, flying directly into a strong wind, so my speed was reduced from about 25 mph to probably 10 mph. My hand really started sweating and I started dropping slowly. The problem was that I was wearing a heavy rig, and if I landed in the water I was going under. My fingers were slipping.

At moments like that you don't think, Boy, this is a great adventure. I can't wait to share this with my family. In fact, this was when I thought, What the hell am I doing here? And then I thought, How did I get into this? And most important, How am I going to get out of this? My hand was barely holding on to the throttle. If I'd had the guts I would have let go and regrasped it before the motor cut out.

I didn't have the guts. I was literally holding down the handle with my little finger. Until that moment I never realized how much strength I had in that finger. It took approximately forever to get across the Ohio frigging River. Finally I saw the landing area. I was looking for smoke or flags to see which way the wind was blowing, but I saw no indication. I also didn't see any power lines or river, so I knew I could figure it out. I watched as the other members of the team made smooth landings and followed their lead.

As soon as my feet were safely on the ground, this terrifying experience suddenly became a great adventure.

I don't know why I put myself in these positions, but I have been doing it throughout my life. I know I am an intelligent man, but I don't necessarily think things through. I just go. I do know people who go through life in a completely different fashion. When facing a decision they begin by going to the end and guessing what the worst possible outcome might be — and then they make decisions based on that. If the forecast is heavy rain they don't leave the house because they are afraid the roads might be dangerous. They hesitate to make a plane reservation several months in advance because it might be snowing that day. There are people who lead a cautious life. But to me, that's like going through life with the emergency brake on.

When nature calls, these people respond by explaining it must have been the wrong number. When nature calls me, I answer. It isn't always the smartest thing to do, but it is who I am.

I can't put myself in their shoes. We all have the opportunity to make that decision: Do I stay in this comfortable situation or do I emerge into the sunlight where I am vulnerable? How much risk am I willing to take? That really is the question. It has been my experience that most human beings would say, "I can't take the risk because I don't know how it is going to turn out, so I am going to stay with what I know." For those people, that is the right decision. Ironically, they may well be more comfortable in their own skin than I am in mine. I have gone through life questing after change and adventure. I still do. Comfort and predictability have never been sufficient for me. At the conclusion of the wonderful movie *Tender Mercies,* Robert Duval is tending a garden, settled with the woman he loves, when she asks him why he seems so unhappy. He looks at her and explains, "I don't trust happiness."

It's not that I don't trust happiness; it just has always been so difficult for me to find. I am as happy as any human being for short periods of time. I revel in good company and great food, in stimulation of many kinds, but then I need more. It revitalizes me, renews me, keeps me going.

I have traveled extensively throughout the world. I am duomoed out. If I never see another reliquary I will be satisfied. I think to myself, You know what, I would be quite content just sitting at home by the pool with Liz, reading a book, watching television, working on my various projects, eating the best Thai food in the universe, and playing with my dogs. That would make me happy. But then the phone rings and someone asks if I would like to fly thirty hours to Cape Town, South Africa. My whole spirit lights up with joy. Weeks later, I am sixteen hours into a flight asking myself how I got there.

One reason for that, I'm certain, is that I am aware of the passage of time and so I push myself and, sometimes, push others, too. I know I have a limited schedule ahead of me, so I don't want to miss anything. So I push, I go, I do. One night in Africa I was sleeping in a hut and I heard sounds outside. Several elephants were passing through. Although we had been warned not to leave the safety of our huts I followed them in the night. They went to the river. I stood there in the brush watching them. I did not think, I'm William Shatner; nothing can happen to me. I didn't sense danger. It was a joyous moment, watching these strange and beautiful creatures; it was that feeling of being completely alive.

Alive, as I was told the next day, at least temporarily. Following wild animals in the jungle at night is very dangerous. Now who could have figured that out? Elephants especially are very protective animals and they will attack. But I couldn't help myself.

I can't stop pushing myself to the edges of my life. I once drove cross-country, from Philadelphia to L.A., stopping in Indianapolis to pick up Liz, who was with her mother. I was driving my Porsche. When you are in a car built for speed there really is only one thing you want to know: How fast will this thing go? I have driven a car 190 mph, but that was on a NASCAR track in a car built for that situation. As I was driving my Porsche through the Allegheny Mountains on my way to Indiana, I began pushing down on the accelerator. And down. I got the car up to 140 mph. Why did I do it? Because I could. There is no other reasonable explanation. It was a silly thing to do. I didn't know much about the car; would a tire explode at that speed? What if I got stopped? That much speeding is a felony, and in many places you will go to jail for it. After picking up Liz, I told her about it. "It was an incredible experience," I said. "You won't believe it."

Talking about it wasn't sufficient, I needed to share that feeling with her. I found the right place on Highway 40 in Oklahoma. There was nobody around and I pushed the car again. This time I got it up to 145 mph.

Liz knows me well enough not to ask, "Is that the best you can do?" We settled for

145 mph. There are people who ask, "How could you have done that? Don't you know your life is at stake?" And my response was always, "How could I have not done it? My life was at stake."

As I've learned, my sense of adventure isn't limited to purely physical experimentation. It's difficult for me to discuss drugs in a society in which addiction is a widespread and serious issue. And let me make it clear that I am not advocating drug use in any way. I have seen the damage that addiction can do. I watched it destroy my marriage and cause Nerine's death. But my curiosity has extended into drugs. It's nearly impossible to be in the entertainment world and not be around drugs. I was born before marijuana was made an illegal drug. I didn't know anything about it until after the United States had passed a law making it illegal — and did so after making alcohol legal once again. The irony is that I have seen alcohol responsible for the death of someone I dearly loved, but I've never seen marijuana hurt anyone — yet marijuana is illegal and alcohol is a huge and profitable business.

I used to smoke pot or grass or weed or whatever it is currently called. I enjoyed it. A friend of mine had a party every Saturday night and there was always pot there. I would go to those parties and get stoned. One Saturday night, as we were sitting there being stoned, someone brought up a news story we had all read: A Korean fisherman had been in the ocean when his boat capsized. He was treading water, preparing himself to die, when he felt something under his feet. It was a porpoise, who literally took him to land and saved his life. Then someone asked, "If you were in the middle of the ocean and you were treading water, and you stepped on something — would you stay there or would you be screaming?"

At that moment that was funniest thing I had ever heard. I could not stop laughing. I was laughing so hard I could barely catch my breath. And the next morning I remembered laughing as hard as I have ever laughed, but I couldn't remember why I was laughing. The following Saturday night I asked, "What was that story again?" And then I start laughing again. That went on for several weeks; each time I got hysterical. But the next morning I couldn't remember the story.

So I've had some good moments with marijuana. I haven't smoked it in a long time. Several years ago I was asked to host a show on the benefits of marijuana and I was hesitant to do it. After a lot of thought, I turned it down. But subsequent to that I did my own research on its benefits, marijuana with THC, marijuana without THC, the oils, all the different variations. I didn't find anything negative. I believe that as we become better educated about it, it will become a useful medical tool. Personally, I liked the feeling.

I've tried other drugs, too. For a time cocaine was everywhere in L.A. I've tried it about a dozen times believing there must be something to it that I'm missing, and I thought it was awful. It didn't make me feel good at all; besides, it made my nose run. In fact, not only didn't it make me feel good, it also was a downer. It really depressed me. I didn't see any reason to continue trying this stuff that made me feel bad.

Over my lifetime I have tried several different drugs. Once I was working in London and had a few days off, so Liz and I decided to go to Amsterdam. I had never been to Holland and wanted to see this great city, and I was also intrigued by the availability of drugs there. This was during the winter and there were very few tourists. We were in a coffee shop and we were offered magic mushrooms. Magic mushrooms? How could I say no? Somewhere in the recesses of my mind I remember reading that *Alice in Wonderland* was actually the description of a psychedelic trip. Well, I always loved *Alice in Wonderland,* and if it were possible to visit Wonderland that appealed to me.

So Liz and I bought the mushrooms and took them as we were told. Then we decided it would be best to be in our hotel room when whatever was going to happen, happened. As we were walking back through streets with women standing behind glass doors and windows, and drug dealers approaching us, I said to Liz, "It's the middle of winter and we're the only tourists here. All of these people are depending on you and me to supply them. We are the bottom fish here."

It took some time for the mushrooms to take effect. For a little while nothing happened. I knew a man who went to Barbados and spent $100 to buy grass — and the dealer sold him grass. Real grass. I wondered if I had bought real mushrooms. But by the time we got back to our room the mushrooms were just beginning to take effect. It came onto me slowly, but when it hit me full force it was terrifying. My experience started with grotesque figures coming out of the walls. This wasn't *The Twilight Zone,* there was no gremlin ripping apart the wing of an airplane, this was a hotel room in Amsterdam, and I had taken something that let loose the monsters. They were, in every way except reality, real to me.

I had never experienced anything like it. The hotel room's walls had become porous and these grotesque creatures were oozing out of them. There was no comic book appearance to them; these were real. I reached over to Liz and my arms began extending and kept growing longer and longer. I can't describe what I was feeling as terrified; it was beyond that. I was frightened by these apparitions, but I was also mystified and fascinated. For me, one of my great fears has always been losing control of my fate, and I was losing control. The thing that kept me securely anchored to reality was the knowledge that Liz was sitting on the bed right next to me, no matter how far away that seemed to be. Finally I said to her, "Are you okay?"

"I am," she replied in an almost dreamy voice. "Isn't this the most beautiful thing you have ever seen!"

It was only then that I discovered she was on a completely different trip. For me, it was all monsters and dangers; for Liz, it was world peace. She told me she saw harmony and gentleness, a world of swirling colors. Her experience was beauty; mine was chaos. I went to the bottom of my soul: My greatest fear is dying, and this experience brought my mind to that place. My fear of death is lurking not far from the surface, and whatever else this touched, it took me there. I didn't want to go back. I wanted to go as far as possible away from that place.

I haven't touched a psychedelic since that day. As I learned, when your mind is altered you can go to a beautiful place or an ugly place. Again, for me, and only for me, I'm glad I did this. What I learned mostly from this experience was that I didn't want to experience it again.

It is amazing to be able to have reached my age and be able to say that I have no regrets about the adventures that I've taken. I've certainly experienced fear; I've hung from a mountain wondering how I was ever going to be able to get up or down. I've stood motionless on a glacier without another human being in sight, too scared to move and counting the seconds until the helicopter reappeared. I've seen the most brutal poverty and the greatest wealth. And through it all I have only a few regrets: My greatest regret is that I once was a hunter and I killed beautiful animals. I don't know how I could have done that; I can't relate to the mind-set necessary to set out to kill a living animal because it makes you feel powerful or successful. It chills me inside when I think about the pain I inflicted. So that's one regret. And second, I regret saying no to potential adventures. That's the irony; I have absolutely no regrets over those things I did and I still remember and wonder about those opportunities I turned down.

More than two decades ago I was invited to join a photographic safari to Antarctica. The plan was to meet a photographer from *National Geographic* in Patagonia and from there take a boat to Antarctica, where we would do a photo essay on penguins. Penguins! I love penguins. Everybody loves penguins. And we were going to shoot them with a camera! This was about a year after Nerine had died and I had recently started dating Liz.

I wanted to go, but I did not want to go to a desolate place alone. I knew I would have too much time to think about Nerine, and when I did my thoughts went to a terrible place. When the magazine gave me permission to bring someone with me, I invited Liz. We didn't really know each other very well. I told her about the trip and assured her that she would have her own cabin. "It's the adventure of a lifetime," I told her.

She was a widow running a horse business in Santa Barbara. She decided to make a list, writing down the pros and cons. After a few days she told me there were more cons than pros and that she had decided not to go.

"How could you turn down a great adventure?" I asked, just before I called the sponsor of the trip to tell them I wasn't going. I regret that decision, although at the time it probably was the right one. I just couldn't bear the thought of being in the middle of an extraordinary adventure in Antarctica and having no one in my life to share it with. I would have been overwhelmed by sadness and despondency.

And every once in a while Liz will say to me, "Wouldn't that have been a wonderful trip?"

So my regrets are for those things I didn't do, rather than the risks I took.

My adventures have often put me in danger. Elephants are known to attack when threatened. Many people have fallen off mountains and glaciers have crevasses. Motorcycle accidents are common. An unexpected wind can throw a kite well off course. Driving 145 miles an hour certainly is risky. And while I have suffered bumps and bruises and cuts I really only have been injured once.

I fell off a horse. "Fell" probably is the wrong word. What happened was that I was riding and as I reached for my hat the horse suddenly spun around and drove me into the ground. I hit the ground hard. I checked my arms and my legs; I turned my head to make sure all the pieces still worked. After I reassured myself that I could still move, the pain hit. I had fractured my upper thigh, which is incredibly painful. It is an area of the body that doctors can't splint. It actually isn't necessary; your leg muscles tighten up around the area to create a natural splint; and they prevent it from moving. The pain emanates from the immobilized muscles. Getting out of bed in the morning was so painful I would start sweating, but I did my best to conduct myself like my leg wasn't broken. The show must go on, and it did. When I had to walk I limped; when it was necessary I used a wheelchair. The physical pain was as intense as anything I had ever experienced.

I could not wait to get back on a horse. I knew how important it was to ride as soon as I could, rather than allowing fear to prevent me from doing that activity I love so much. It was several weeks before I could manage it, and admittedly there was some trepidation. My leg was healing and I had been warned that if it should be reinjured before it healed completely the damage would be much more severe. But I couldn't resist.

It took months before all the stiffness was gone and I was riding naturally again.

I believe that everybody has an element of that voyage of exploration in them. And I think it behooves you to take tentative steps to see what that exploration can bring you. We all fight a continuous battle between comfort and adventure, security and risk. Taking a chance always is dangerous, and we never know for sure where it will lead us. On one hand, there is the passionate person who decides to go into the heart of Africa to find Dr. Livingstone; conversely, there is the father of a young child who doesn't want to take unnecessary risks because he needs to do whatever is necessary to keep a roof over his child's head.

I have the luxury of saying yes because I have a secure base. My life is paid for. My family's future is secured. I am able to put myself in harm's way, but I do so knowing the odds are strongly in my favor. For many people, though, security is far more important than risking new experiences. It is very human to cling to those rocks of security.

But just living life can be dangerous. You may walk out the door and be hit by a car. A piano might fall on your head. A cosmic ray may zip through your body and alter your DNA. Life doesn't come with a double-your-money-back hundred-year guarantee. Security often is less secure than we like to believe it is.

I am not advocating that you try parasailing or dancing on glaciers or climbing mountains. I'm certainly not suggesting you drive halfway across the country in a snowstorm or try psychedelic drugs. What I am suggesting is that once in a while you take yourself out of your comfort zone. Adventure has very different meanings to people. Several years ago I interviewed the Canadian astronaut Chris Hadfield as he orbited Earth in a capsule. That was his day job. And prior to that he was a test pilot, who had spent years testing new equipment — the kind of equipment that, had it failed, could have killed him. But he had another passion; he wanted to be a singer. And years after that interview I found myself onstage with him as he played a guitar and sang. He told me that day how nervous he was to sing in front of an audience.

For him, that was an adventure. Risking his life had been his job, but singing in front of a live audience took real courage.

We can all set our sails for our next adventure, even if we never lose sight of the lighthouse.

7.
WORKING TO FIND HAPPINESS

I have never had a guru. I have never had someone I could turn to for sage advice. I have climbed mountains; I have wandered through jungles; I have been all over the world. I have looked for him. Or her. And I can report now without any hesitation: There is no guru with the secret to happiness.

I've found that too many people spend a great deal of time searching for happiness, rather than simply being happy.

As I got older I came to an astonishing realization: I was happy. It wasn't something I had planned or actively pursued, but I definitely was happy. With that realization, I began asking other people their secrets to finding happiness in their lives. Most of them fumbled a bit, mentioned they hadn't really thought about it, then hee-hawed (I have a lot of country-western friends), and finally confided in me their own method.

Adding what I was told to my own experience, it can be summed up rather simply: To be happy in life, do those things that make you happy and don't do those things that make you unhappy.

The problem with that, Bill, I suspect many readers are responding, is that four-letter word: work. Too often work gets in the way of happiness. We all have to do it. This should be the place where I would mention what percentage of your life you spend working. As there is no single statistic I can quote that would make me sound authoritative, I'll make one up from the Bureau of Alternative Facts: Of necessity, we spend a substantial amount of our lives working. Sometimes substantial plus overtime!

Most of us work to survive. We tend to see it as what we have to do to pay for those things we want to do. "Work" occupies a significant amount of time in our lives. For some people it takes up the most time. So how then to equate doing those things that make you happy with being forced to work? For many people that is a far more difficult problem to solve than the Yang–Mills existence and mass gap.

Let me point something out to you. What do the wealthiest people in America do every day? People such as Bill Gates, Mike Bloomberg, and Warren Buffett? They go to work is what they do. These are people who have earned more money than they can ever possibly spend. The last thing they have to do is work. They could go fishing or gardening or bowling and never have to worry about paying the mortgage. And yet they continue to work. These people have figured out how to find satisfaction and pleasure from their work.

The real difficulty here comes in defining work. In our society, work has come to mean doing a job. People get up in the morning and go to work to do their job. That's not what I am referring to when I talk about work. A job can be work, of course, but work is not necessarily your job. Some people are fortunate enough to be able to find great pleasure in their job. Many people don't, though, and they have to find it in other places. Later in Leonard Nimoy's life, for example, after he had retired from acting, he started working — working — full-time on his photography and his poetry. Creating art became his work. There is a reason an artist's output is referred to as "works of art" or his "body of work." Leonard's *Full Body Project,* for example, which celebrated large-sized women, came about, he said, because "I'm troubled by the fact that women in our culture are congratulated most for losing weight." His accomplishments as a photographer and poet brought him tremendous satisfaction, perhaps more than he ever got from acting.

Communicating thoughts and ideas through his words and images was his work. For me, work is the sustenance of my life. It is my work that keeps me moving forward and from which I continue to draw satisfaction and pride. My accomplishments make me feel good. They remind me that even at my age I am still a contributing member of society, that I am able to meet new challenges, and that more adventures are to come. In my case, what I refer to as my work isn't limited to acting. I work with my horses, trying to perfect my riding ability as well as their skills. I work with my dogs, breeding and training. I work with several charities. I work trying to use what power I have gained from my success in the entertainment world in other forums. My work, whatever it is that day, that moment, adds joy and excitement to my life and keeps me involved in the world. I don't have any doubt that having that kind of focus can extend your life: Pablo Picasso was still hard at work when he died at ninety-one years old. Work, as I refer to it here, means simply a central and meaningful focus of your life. A reason to be excited when you wake up in the morning.

I was happy, I realized, because I love what I do. I don't love it every minute, I don't love every aspect of it, I don't love getting up at 5:00 A.M., I don't love the distractions and the issues, but I have found enormous pleasure in my work. Incredibly, to me being busy working all day is almost erotic. I get a kind of sexual pleasure from it, not quite as vivid as making love, but it brings me such joy. For me, it is the ecstasy of life. I know my wife feels that way when she is working with horses. I know people who feel this same way when they are working in their garden; I know songwriters who feel that way when they are struggling with a tune. I know auto and motorcycle mechanics who can get lost in the bliss of a roaring engine. I know teachers who take tremendous pride in the success of their most difficult students. I know carpenters, and fitness instructors, and chess players, I know writers and party planners and comedians, who derive tremendous pleasure from their work — and never stop trying to be better at it.

I no longer have to work. The mortgage is paid. But in the spring of 2017 I starred in a movie titled *Senior Moment.* It was shot on a location three hours outside L.A. With some minor difficulty, I could have commuted. But I decided to stay in the area by myself. More than a year earlier I had been in Halifax, Nova Scotia, at the beginning of winter making an extended appearance on the TV series *Haven.*

It was a very difficult situation: I was staying in a somewhat moldy hotel that featured remarkably bad food and we were shooting in a warehouse that had been converted into a sound stage. "Converted" is not quite accurate: No sound baffling had been done, it had a tin roof which magnified the thump of raindrops hitting it, and it had no glass windows. Oh, it also had limited heat. We were shooting in one of the dampest and coldest places on Earth where people actually try to live. In November. It was so cold in the studio that when we weren't on the set we stayed inside tents next to the electric heaters. The camerapersons had to figure out how to shoot scenes supposedly taking place indoors without showing the condensation from each breath. It was awful.

I loved it. Well, perhaps I loved it more in retrospect. For the four weeks I was there I was totally enshrouded in the veil of work. I would leave my hotel gladly early in the morning to be driven to this icebox of a studio, stay near the heater until I was called, perform as long as I was needed, which usually was early morning to late at night, then make my way back to this soggy hotel.

It was a very difficult shoot. I focused on the work. I didn't call home; I didn't talk to my children; I did what I needed to do for that one cold month in early winter in Halifax.

I didn't have to do it. I could just as easily have been out there having fun in the warm California sun with my family, my horses, and my dogs. But I couldn't not do it. I have always derived tremendous pleasure from working. I like being challenged, I like the feeling of accomplishment I get for doing a job well, and I like the pride I take in simply getting a hard job done. It makes me feel useful, like I'm still in the game.

I enjoyed that difficult experience so much that when I was offered the romantic lead (let me repeat that for my own pleasure, when I was offered the romantic lead . . .) in a movie titled *Senior Moment* I approached it as I had the Halifax experience. I lived like a monk in a lovely hotel, eating nuts and figs and focusing on nothing but the movie.

People ask me why I did that. My answer is, Why not? The opportunity was there to do something I truly enjoyed. More than that, within days of the end of that shoot I flew to Europe to work with Henry Winkler, Terry Bradshaw, George Foreman, and young comedian Jeff Dye on the second season of a reality show titled *Better Late Than Never*. For this show, billed as "an international adventure in hope of having a life-changing experience," we traipse around Asia and Europe having unscripted adventures. I was there for six more weeks.

Why not?

Just like everybody else, I have been working my entire life. I started working on a radio program when I was six years old and just never stopped. I never saw a reason to stop. There was never anything I wanted to do more than what I was doing. In some ways I have been a workaholic. I rarely go to Hollywood parties or spend hours just relaxing. For me, working is my relaxation. If I'm not performing or writing or being with my horses or dogs I am busy planning the next projects in my head. I am putting pieces together, trying to recruit people to bring my concepts into fruition. There is always a performance of some kind going on in my head, ideas presenting themselves for approval or dismissal, words at play, questions to be answered. It doesn't stop, nor would I want it to stop. Actually, in all ways I am a workaholic.

Some of my work consisted of jobs I took because I needed the salary. But the only job I've ever done outside entertainment consisted of delivering orders to customers in cars at an Orange Julius in Montreal. I was not even a waiter, I was a server, and I wasn't very good at it. I don't remember why I took that job — I was earning a stipend for performing on local radio — but I did. The job description was basic: take this order to that car.

I like to believe I approached that job with my usual enthusiasm. But perhaps it would have been smarter to approach it with more focus. My second day on the job I tripped off a curb and dumped an entire order, including that deliciously refreshing Orange Julius drink, through an open car window. There isn't much to be said when you fail at delivering a tray. I do remember taking a streetcar home, probably realizing my career in the service industry was over.

And also like everybody else I have had to work at jobs I did not like at all. I have done commercials that I knew I shouldn't be doing. I have been in movies and TV shows that I knew I shouldn't be doing. I have forgotten most of them, perhaps the only advantage of growing older, but they were mostly innocuous things that people hadn't heard of or aren't aware of, films and shows that failed and were forgotten or were never released. Projects that exist only on IMDb and usually draw the response "I never heard of that. I wonder what that one is about?" Here's a suggestion: Don't wonder; there is a reason you never heard about it.

I think every actor has these projects on their résumé. But there was one project that stands out as perhaps the silliest thing I have ever done. Among the movies and TV shows and books and records and concerts and all the rest, this is one I will never forget: I did a stand-up comedy act as Captain Kirk. It was an act that will live in infamy. It fell into the category "it seemed like a good idea at the time."

I have done many live performances. I have luxuriated in the warmth of an audience's laughter. I know how to tell a story to draw the largest response. That's my job and my work. But this was different. I was performing the entire act in the character of James T. Kirk. I can't recall why I did it or, mercifully, the material that I used. There was no "Spock and Bones walked into a transporter." What I do remember is an entire audience staring at me with their mouths open in awe as we all realized we were in the middle of a complete disaster and there was no way to stop it. No one laughed with me or at me. They were as stunned as I was at this colossally bad idea. At least with bad movies, TV shows, or albums I didn't have to look directly at an audience. Here I had no choice. But I kept going. This was one of those it-wasn't-funny-at-the-time situations, which actually might be the worst possible way of reviewing a stand-up comedy routine.

But I kept going. I've never considered what my eulogy might be, but "He kept going" would not be bad. At times we all have to do work we don't enjoy. Every career, like every life, is cyclical. No one goes through life in neutral. There are going to be great moments and stand-up moments. The question is what do you do when you find yourself in that situation? I kept going. I knew that performance was going to end or that TV show was going to be forgotten. I knew time would pass and with luck it would be forgotten. So I did the best job I could at that time while continuing to search for opportunities to do other things that I would enjoy more.

I know there are people caught in jobs they hate that they have to keep doing to pay their rent or support their family. The best advice I can give to people in that situation is to find a book that gives them better advice. This book isn't it. This book is about what I have learned, and by the nature of my profession I have never been in that situation. My jobs end naturally. The movie is done. The show goes off the air. The audience responds. The Priceline negotiator drives off a cliff.

But when I have found myself caught in a bad situation, I have tried to find ways of making it at least palatable. The first thing I did was the best that I could. I had to perform and eliminate any negative thoughts about the situation. I couldn't allow my anger or bitterness to erode my performance. I did the best I could. I learned to ignore both the emotional and physical pain and focus only on what I had to do in the moment. The ability to do that would seem to be a gift, but it isn't; it is something I have learned how to do through experience.

In many instances the cause of the problem is other people. The work, the job, might be tolerable, but you are forced to work with people who don't want to be there and take out their anger and frustrations on everyone around them. I have experienced that several times. I know the wrong way to handle it: I punched out a cast member onstage, which probably demonstrated a lack of restraint on my part — although admittedly it did feel great. We were in a scene that called for him to slap me on the back. Depending on whether or not he got a laugh from an earlier line, he would slap me hard or soft. I warned him that he was hitting me too hard. I complained to the producer, to Actors' Equity, to anyone who would listen, and I told him the next time he did it I was going to deck him. I did.

That was one way to deal with the situation. I would not recommend that.

When I was in the play *The World of Suzie Wong,* our Suzie Wong didn't want to be there. Our leading lady was a beautiful young Asian woman. It apparently never occurred to anyone that the fact that she barely spoke English might be a problem. Eventually, she wanted to get out of her contract. In my opinion, she did everything possible to sabotage the show. She would forget her lines; she would miss her cues; she would wander offstage and not come back. It was the actor's nightmare come true. For the two years I was in that play with her, I would walk through the stage door fearful of what might happen onstage that night. Instead of reveling in the fact that my name was above the title on a Broadway theater marquee I was angry and confused and terrified.

The situation was even worse. The Rodgers and Hammerstein musical *Flower Drum Song* had opened about the same time we did and some of the newly formed suburban theater groups confused the two shows and mistakenly bought tickets for *The World of Suzie Wong.* We were sold out for almost two years. I had signed a run-of-play contract. So no matter how bad the show was, I was stuck in it for two years. When the curtain rose and no one broke out into a big raucous opening number, members of the audience initially were confused, then often dismayed. Occasionally hostile.

And then they had to sit through what at times became a shambles. I was onstage for most of the play. When the show fell apart it left me exposed. To the audience it appeared I was the one who had forgotten my lines or my actions. The audience didn't know that the half of the play who did not speak English was offstage refusing to come on. I kept going. I did the best I could. Whenever possible, I got a laugh.

It was not funny at that time. I was at the beginning of my career and I was looking at the end of my career. This was supposed to be an important step in building my career; instead the building was collapsing. As difficult as it was for me, I never missed a performance. I showed up, I did my job to the best of my ability, and I remained hopeful that this would lead to a better situation.

No matter what it is you are doing, there always are going to be hurdles to be overcome. That's part of the challenge; it also makes success more enjoyable. I only worked with Roger Corman once. Roger Corman was the master of B movies. It is impossible to know how many people began their careers working with him. I'm not sure that he was ecstatic about the movies he made, but he kept making them. His budgets were below minimal and he became a genius at doing things inexpensively; cutting corners is not a good thing, because it leads to cutting quality. But sometimes it becomes necessary just to get things done. Roger just wanted to get it on film, although that "it" was sometimes pretty dubious.

Corman always referred to the movie we did together as the only movie on which he lost money, and although I have the feeling he told that to many people, he also called it the best movie he ever made. And many years later it finally became profitable.

Budget versus quality was a battle we fought every day on *Star Trek.* On that set the lights went out at 6:12 whatever we were doing and that was it. There was no money in the budget for overtime. Six twelve, done. The production company had to do it that way because that was the dictate of the studio. The studio had to do it that way because the network wouldn't pay anything additional. So the fish was stinking from the top and it made its way all the way down to the makeup artist or the quality of the food served by craft services. Not that craft services was feeding us rotten fish, of course. (Here's an aside to young actors: Never, ever criticize craft services.)

By the time we got to our third season, when our already tiny budget was cut again, our goal became to see if we could get it done well as well as getting it done fast. That was our most difficult season but at least in some ways the most enjoyable because we were all fighting the same enemy. No matter what hurdles were put in our way, we got over them by 6:12.

We did whatever we could to make an

often unpleasant situation enjoyable. We played practical jokes on one another, we formed a loose alliance against "the suits," and we did the best possible job under the circumstances. There have been many millions of words written about *Star Trek.* I believe it is fair to say that no show in TV history has been more analyzed, criticized, or memorialized than *Star Trek.* I have read much of it. I've even written some of it. But I don't recall ever seeing anyone claiming that the actors gave anything less than the best of their ability.

In my life this is simply another example of what at the moment appeared to be a disaster that instead became a rose. The result of our commitment to doing the best job we could in circumstances we all despised was something none of us could ever anticipate. We were doing our jobs, in some cases showing up for the desperately needed paycheck; we did not have the slightest suspicion we were making entertainment history. It never occurred to any of us that standing there holding cheap plastic guns and talking to rocks would eventually lead to long and successful careers. That's really the message: Even under the worst circumstances do the very best job of which you are capable, because you never know who is watching you. In our case, literally. And you never know what it might lead to.

That certainly was not the only time in my career that I found myself wondering what I was doing there and waiting impatiently for 6:12 so I could go home. But my response in each of those situations was the same: Doing the best possible job. No matter what was happening around me. No matter if my costar refused to say her lines or another actor was punching me or I was making a movie in a language even I didn't speak, I did the best job I was capable of doing and somehow it all worked out just fine.

I don't know a lot of people who have retired and lived happily ever after. General MacArthur once said, "Old soldiers never die; they just fade away." A similar thing might be said about actors: "Old actors never die: they just fade to black." The people I have known in the entertainment industry have kept working as long as someone was willing to hire them. There is an old actors' joke:

"I had a man ask me just yesterday if I had thought about retiring."

"Really? That's great. Who was it?"

"The director."

The thought of retiring has never occurred

to me. I know how fortunate I am that I am still being asked to do the job I've spent my life training to do. And, honestly, I think I am better at it now than I have ever been in my life. It's taken me most of eighty years, but I've finally figured out how to do my job and I love doing it. And I intend to keep doing it as long as I am able. I am one of those very lucky people who is never going to retire.

No one should retire when their work remains pleasurable. What would I do if I retired? That's the question I would ask anyone, whether they are a nuclear physicist or a laborer. If your job isn't pleasant I understand the need to change, but retiring to sit on the back porch and rock will atrophy not only your body but also your mind, and it will do it within months. Personally, I have no reason to retire. I would end up doing exactly what I am doing now. I am one of those very fortunate people. I have spent my life doing work I loved, even when I didn't love the job I was doing. People may retire from a job, but I don't believe they should stop working.

My wife, Elizabeth, for example, was a wonderful horse trainer with her late husband. We met in that world. But after we married, being together meant that she could no longer continue that profession. So her work became taking care of us. In fact, although she sort of retired, she probably is busier than previously. She takes care of both of our schedules, makes certain that what needs to be done in my life is done, and takes care of our home and our immediate and extended families. She has become one of the primary professional judges in several different types of horse competitions. She has continued to ride and train a few horses and she has begun doing photography. Although she has no job she has to go to, she never stops working. And it seems to make her very happy.

When I write about the importance of work, that's what I mean. Find that thing or those things you enjoy doing and do them. It doesn't have to be a paid position, it might be volunteer work, or a hobby; it makes no difference. It's that thing that you look forward to doing. A purpose to your day. That something from which you derive satisfaction.

Age isn't a barrier. You can begin something at eighty-six and work at it. A good deal of my time is spent beginning new projects. Just after I celebrated my eighty-sixth birthday, for example, I read some beautiful poetry a military veteran had sent me and realized it could be the basis of a one-man show. In my mind I saw the finished product. It needed music and some minor staging, it certainly would take more than a year to produce it. I got very excited about it; I began trying to figure out which musicians might want to work with me developing it. As these thoughts ran through my mind I became energized.

Will it ever get done? Perhaps, but many years ago I saw a segment of the great Charles Kuralt's "On the Road" series that obviously made an impact on me. A retired Wright, Minnesota, dairy farmer named Gordon Bushnell believed there should be a direct two-hundred-mile highway from Duluth to Fargo, so he set out to build it — by himself, with only a wheelbarrow, a shovel, and an old tractor. He was having some health problems, but as he discovered, "I started working, and the more I worked the better I felt. And the pain went away. . . . There's fellas have retired — younger than I am — that go and sit down and listen to TV, and they're dead."

He worked on that highway for twenty years, completing nine miles when the piece was done. He was seventy-eight years old and had 191 miles to go. Obviously he would never complete it, but as Kuralt said,

Bushnell had discovered that "it wasn't the road that mattered; it was building the road."

You have to build your own road, or nurture your own plants, or even chase Terry Bradshaw with a rotten fish. It is essential for your physical and mental well-being. If you're a technician of any kind and you have computer skills, then sit down and work at that computer. If you have people skills, those don't go away. Even if you have physical impairments that can be overcome to some extent, do what you can do. Challenge yourself. I know someone who began playing a guitar in his sixties. It was too late for him to fulfill his youthful ambition of becoming a rock star, but he worked at it. He improved. He learned how to play new chords and came close to making music. It wasn't being a rock star that mattered; it was seeing himself getting a little bit better at the guitar every day that mattered.

He set a challenge for himself, learned to play the guitar, and trying to meet that challenge continues to bring him great pleasure. Work within your limitations, but work. Don't sit in front of the TV set, unless of course you're watching a show in which I'm involved, and let your life slip by without your even noticing it.

The fact that I don't know how not to work has been a great blessing for me. It has kept me actively involved in life throughout my entire life. My suggestion is that you respond to anyone who asks what makes you happy with, "I'm working at it."

8.
RELATIONSHIPS ARE NOT ALL RELATIVE

"Alone."

What a painful word this is for me. It carries with it so much meaning: Isolation. Estrangement. Abandonment. Loneliness. And fear.

I don't believe living things are meant to go through life alone. That has been an important lesson for me, although admittedly at times I have struggled to form relationships. It's not something at which I have been especially skilled. I think by nature we are programmed to both want and need the companionship of others, in a great variety of forms. I think living things are all connected in some incredible way. We are all little electrical stations, our bodies giving off electrical waves. We have the technology to communicate electronically with satellites at the end of our solar system, so it is difficult for me to believe that we don't feel those electrical vibrations emanating from someone standing right next to us. Perhaps we simply lack the means of interpreting them.

There is evidence that some of us are able to connect on some level other than consciousness with others. People who live together find that they often have similar thoughts at the same time: "I knew you were going to say that." Or we think about someone and that person calls us, saying, "I was just thinking about you." I don't think this is a coincidence, or an accident; I think our little radio stations are simply receiving each other. I have been working with my assistant, Kathleen Hays, for more than six years. After working together often more than twelve hours a day, week after week, we certainly have learned to anticipate each other. It also isn't limited to human beings. On the most fundamental level, scientists have measured low-energy signals moving from tree to tree; they have evidence of trees displaying a response when trees around them are cut down.

I know I am able to communicate with my dogs. My dogs know what I am thinking, obviously in the most general terms, and respond to it. When I need them by me after a trying time they are there. They just are there. I don't invite them, or call them;

they sense somehow they are needed and they respond. Anyone who has had an animal knows that to be true, that animals have an innate ability to understand human needs and, in many cases, how to fulfill them.

We are all vibrating, I believe, sending out electrical signals to those other living things capable of receiving and deciphering them. Those signals are energy; I describe them as the energy of life. And I do believe that there are certain people, the people we call holy men, who simply are in tune with the rest of us. On the highest level that vibration, to me, is passion. But then something else takes over, love, friendship, appreciation, respect. And all of it connects us to the world; it connects us to other people.

We simply were not created to be alone. In the movie *Cast Away,* for example, Tom Hanks found it absolutely essential to form a relationship with a volleyball. People who have chosen or been forced to spend considerable time by themselves often end up creating invisible beings with whom they have a semblance of a relationship. Once, when I was with my family in Hawaii, I saw what appeared to be a body lying on the beach, roped off with yellow police crime scene tape. When I asked a policeman what had happened, he replied it was nothing, he was protecting a monk seal. While seals generally live in colonies, a monk seal stays by itself, hence the name. Once a year monk seals returned to this beach to breed and have their pups.

The following morning, just after dawn, I was swimming in the ocean by myself. It was too early for anyone else to be there. As I was treading water I suddenly felt something grab me from behind and hold on to me. I turned around and looked right into the face of a monk seal. I screamed; I was frightened to death. It had grabbed me with its flippers. The animal looked at me and disappeared; as far as I know it did not return to the beach. The young man putting out the chairs heard me screaming and saw the seal disappear. I told the story at breakfast that morning, but no one believed me. It is true, it happened, and in my mind that monk seal was so alone it craved contact with another living thing. It needed to feel like it wasn't alone.

We are herd animals, most comfortable when we are involved in myriad relationships on all levels, from intimate to peripheral; these are the bonds that bring us together. You can see that by looking at nature. From whales and sharks to bees and ants, most species thrive as a community; in many instances their lives depend on their relationships. We live in the great matrix of relationships that are absolutely necessary for our physical, spiritual, and mental well-being.

It is our relationships that carry us through life. When discussing relationships, many people assume that the most important relationship is romantic love. That's a nice assumption; it's what we have been told our entire lives, but it isn't necessarily true. And, in fact, it may even complicate things. The whole concept of romance and love has been invented. Romantic love didn't exist for thousands of years. Some society, maybe the Greeks or the early Egyptians, created it. But before that the necessity of joining a group of men to hit a mammoth on its head, or wondering whether the saber-toothed tiger was going to steal it from you, then lighting a fire and cooking it, finally going to sleep in a darkened cave, didn't allow for romance.

Nobody gave roses to another person — unless they were edible. When mankind was focused on survival and reproduction there was no time or need for romance. People bonded together and formed relationships because they were more powerful as a tribe.

Romantic love began when mankind had time to dress up and put on all the necessities to attract the other sex. The whole Knights of the Round Table idea, in which men pined and yearned and willingly undertook noble deeds to win the heart of a fair maiden, was a wonderful fairy tale. Fear of mammoths had been replaced by the need for companionship. Then Shakespeare wrote of unbridled romantic love. So it's a comparatively recent invention.

But romance can be perishable. It often doesn't last. We are conditioned by what we see on the stage, in movies, what we read and hear about: to endlessly pursue romance and to believe our life is at least partially barren when we are not involved in some type of romance. Much too often people believe they are incomplete if they are not involved romantically with another person. They go through life feeling empty, feeling like a failure, because they are not attached romantically.

What they fail to understand, what I have learned, is that there are other, maybe even healthier, forms of love and relationships. People generally don't appreciate that because it's not what they are seeing on television or being told on social media. We are constantly barraged with products to make ourselves more enticing to other people. We are continually being told that seemingly everybody else has found that special person and made to feel like failures if we haven't "met cute." But there are so many other types of love: There is friendship, love for animals, for charity, for God. And there are other levels of fulfilling relationships: There are people you work with on a daily basis, people you respect and rely on; there are your neighbors and other people you encounter on a regular basis who add a little enjoyment to your everyday life with their smile, whether it is a teacher or the woman who takes your ticket in the movie theater. We live in a world of relationships of every type and intensity, yet it has been my experience that people often fail to recognize it and they fail to appreciate the importance of all of these relationships. By "people," I mean me too.

Appreciating and fostering relationships is a learned behavior. It doesn't necessarily come naturally or even easily to many people. It's difficult to do, and it took me most of my lifetime to figure that out. The first meaningful relationship in all of our lives is with our parents, and what we take from that relationship will affect us the rest of our lives. Relationships are learned behavior. There are different concepts on how to treat a crying baby. Some parents believe in allowing an infant to cry itself into exhaustion, while others will pick up and comfort the baby every time it makes its presence known. Some mothers are able to read their child's needs and wants very accurately; others simply follow the pre-scribed tried-and-true manner.

I wasn't swaddled. I don't remember com-municating very closely with my mother. My father was working and wasn't present much of the time, so he became a figure of discipline and respect. As a result, I did not have an especially loving bond with my mother. I hear grown men talking about "my mom," or I see professional athletes thanking "Mom." My mother was never a "mom." I've thought about that; my mother came from an old-country background. My tendency is to think of those peasants who spent long hours working in the fields of Europe, which gave them less time for demonstrable love. I think that I'm a prod-uct of that. I think that shaped my life and my relationships.

Your parents' relationships with each other and with their children set the tem-plate for how a loving relationship with another human being, even a marriage, is supposed to work. We know, for example, that children of a wife batterer may end up abusing their own spouses. Abusing someone has become their understanding of love: "He," or "she," "hits me because they love me." Or, conversely, "I love her because I hit her."

My parents were good, decent people who had admirable values, contributed to the world, had friends, and gave to others. My father worked so hard to bring his family to Canada, it was the most important thing to him, yet I don't recall any great displays of great affection between him and his siblings. He worked incredibly hard to provide a better life for them, but interactions were subdued.

Now, my Auntie Pearl, that was a whole different story. I don't quite know what I learned from her, but it must have been considerable because I have a very vivid memory and appreciation for her. Auntie Pearl came from the same background as my mother but was a totally different character. And she was a character; she had the flamboyance of Auntie Mame. Everything she did seemed exotic to me; she married a psychiatrist and moved to California. They had three children and divorced. My mother told me never to talk about that divorce because in those years it was considered shameful.

Auntie Pearlie was ostracized, which never made any sense to me. She was the member of the family with a sense of adventure. She was bright and full of fun and laughter. Both she and my mother had a love of life; the difference was my mother acted it out within her boundaries while Pearlie lived it.

Pearlie and I were both middle children. I grew up with a sister who was three years older than me, Joy, and my other sister Farla, who was eleven years younger than me. I think they got less attention than I did because I was the boy. No older sister wants a younger brother trailing after her, and Farla was so much younger than either of us that we were deeply involved in our adolescent adventures when she was born. Both of my sisters are lovely, nice people who married well. They continued to live in Montreal, and even though we love one another and speak relatively often there is a physical, emotional, and psychological separation from both of my sisters. They are my family, but they have never been intensely in my life.

There is no question in my mind that I took something from each of those relationships. It was as if I had a Chinese restaurant menu of relationships to choose from: my serious and somber hardworking father, my too-often outrageous mother, my flamboyant aunt, my older sister, and our younger sibling. Like Pearl, I left a very conservative, and safe, household, with a secure business I could have gone into, to venture into a world where failure is the norm. But I left home without learning how to form relationships. I had to figure that out through a long series of fumbles and misguided attempts.

One of the earliest relationships I formed was with a prostitute who became my friend. At the time it was not something I valued, but in a lifetime of exciting and unusual experiences, the following incident is one of the few I recall with clarity and shame. It happened almost sixty years ago and yet I remember it well and still feel my discomfort. This is another of the very few regrets I have in my life.

When I first moved from Montreal to Toronto at the very beginning of my career I was living in a fifth-floor walk-up, sleeping on that rope bed. I was looking desperately for any kind of work on television I could find, but it was difficult. There was a hotel nearby that had an attached cafeteria that offered all-you-can-eat meals for two dollars. Whole families, and I, would go there for the cheap food. The cafeteria would close at eight o'clock and after that a large bar opened. That bar became a hangout for prostitutes whose clients would "rent" a room in the hotel. I would eat my two-dollar dinner, then go into the bar and sit with these women. When they had a client they would leave the table for a period of time, then return to rejoin the conversation. I became friendly with several of them. One or two of them allowed me into their bed from time to time. Looking back now, I understand we all were trying to make real contact with another human being. They had their job, I had mine, but on some level we all were looking for companionship. Not sexual, that was the easy part, but rather something far more difficult to find. I was incredibly lonely and these women became my tribe; they helped me survive.

Eventually I had some success. I spent three years performing Shakespeare at Tyrone Guthrie's Stratford Festival. The second year there I met Gloria, and by the end of that season I had asked her to marry me. Months later I was with her and her parents in Toronto. Gloria came from a very proper, successful family. As we came out of a movie theater, I saw one of my friends from the bar coming toward us. From her manner, the way she was dressed, her profession was obvious. I didn't know what to do. Inside, I was panicking. The last thing I wanted was for Gloria's parents to discover I knew this woman. She was a prostitute; what would they think of me? As she passed our eyes met; it was obvious she recognized me. She clearly sized up the situation and neither of us acknowledged the other. We glanced at each other once more, and then she was gone down the street. I took a deep breath, believing that was over, I had gotten away with something.

Over? I have carried my shame with me for the rest of my life. This had been an important relationship to me and I was so desperate for approval that I lacked the courage to admit that. At my age now I would have behaved differently, but I understood my actions as a young man. It was the only thing I was capable of doing. I should have rushed over and embraced her, which would have been very courageous, and maybe explained that I knew that lady several years ago and she helped me. I couldn't; I was so emotionally bound: I was going to get married; I was going to have a real relationship, which meant I was no longer going to be alone. And this was going to be my family. I was so desperate for a relationship that I failed to recognize the importance in my life of that earlier relationship.

As I've written previously, once upon a time I believed deep passionate love was the most powerful type of relationship. That loving someone without conditions was the ultimate goal and that we all spend our lives seeking it. Then I met and married an alcoholic. Because I believed true love conquered everything I had no doubt my true love for Nerine would enable her to conquer her addiction.

I believed that. Boy, was I wrong.

When I look back at my life I am sometimes amazed at those things I did in search of love. But nothing compares to marrying an alcoholic. I went to Al-Anon, the organization for the families and friends of alcoholics, and they tried to teach me how to live with an alcoholic. I told them, "I don't want to live with an alcoholic. I don't have to deal with someone who is drunk. I want her to stop." To me, this was like the movies; in the end my love would overcome everything and the orchestra would play beautiful music as we walked together in our future. It had always worked with my animals; why couldn't it work with her?

I spent most of my life learning these lessons. Like everyone else, I had relationships that I didn't appreciate enough; with Leonard Nimoy, for example. Leonard was the best friend I ever had, and without realizing it I must not have paid sufficient attention to that relationship, because at the end of his life he was no longer speaking to me. Many people refuse to believe this, but I never knew what I had done to cause that; I certainly had never done anything intentionally.

Nerine's death devastated me, but at least I understood what had happened. Until the day I die, though, I will wonder what caused that rift with Leonard. After all the years we had spent together, after the bond we had forged, what could I have done that was so irreparable that he couldn't even talk to me about it?

Actors live transient lives. Unlike many people, we don't go to an office or workplace every day and see the same people and, over time, form relationships. As an actor the more successful you are, the more shallow your roots, because the job involves so much traveling. I am now bound together forever in American cultural history with the cast of *Star Trek*. Often though, people mistake the relationships our characters had during that three-year-long journey for real life. The relationship between Spock and Mc-Coy, the battle between intellect and emotion, for example, was idealized. In fact, we were a group of actors brought together by a producer. The only thing we had in common was that all of us were working actors who had played many different roles. When *Star Trek* was canceled we each continued our careers in different directions, and if we thought about it at all we knew we might bump into each other in completely different roles. It was only long afterward, after the show became a cult hit and then a franchise, that we were brought back together. But that was typical of the type of relationships I had with my fellow actors.

I have always believed that was at least part of the reason I never had any really close friends. By "close friends" I mean the type of relationship so beautifully depicted between Denny Crane and James Spader's Alan Shore on *Boston Legal.* I have had, and do have, many people I like and respect and admire, whom I truly enjoy being with, but these are not the kind of deep friendships in which you can unburden yourself to the other person when necessary. Friends need to share many experiences over a span of time, not one or two seasons or on a movie set. You don't go on a trip and return saying, "I made a good friend." Perhaps you got friendly and talked about mutual interests and ideas and found an enjoyable common ground. I use the word "acquaintance" to describe that relationship. I have had a dearth of those deeper relationships in my lifetime.

I don't know why, although I suspect, I learned as a Jewish boy in Christian Montreal that it was emotionally safer to keep some distance between myself and other people. Have I missed something by not having that level of friendship? I think perhaps so. I remember watching wistfully as the two brothers on our motorcycle trip separated; one of them had to go back to work. They told me they really loved each other, although there were times they didn't like each other. But their bonds were so strong that when one of them left they embraced and cried. I had never had a relationship quite like that.

I had to accept the reality that the most meaningful friendship I had ever had was over. If I were to live my life again I would be far more approachable; I would be more open. I know I put up walls to keep people from getting too close emotionally; I didn't approach people and obviously did not give off the scent that they should approach me. I could have changed that, but I don't think I was fully aware of it. Because of that I have had very few deep and meaningful relationships beyond my family. Looking back on that, I think it is probable I've missed an extra sweetener of life. I should have been more open, but truthfully I didn't know how to be.

Perhaps not surprisingly, I have always been able to form deep relationships with my dogs and horses. Anyone who doubts that the feelings you invest in animals and the rewards you receive in return are not as meaningful as those we give and receive from people must never have had a pet. And just as with a person, relationships have to be made. Every relationship I have had with an animal has been different. I have become much closer with some animals than others. Here's what I learned about relationships from my animals: Forming any relationship begins with communication. I believe any attempt to communicate with another living being is an act of love. You wish to discover. You wish to learn more about them. You wish to impart to that entity your own availability. The end result is, no matter how adept you become at your mutual language, by striving to communicate you have formed the basis of a relationship. The more successful you are in establishing any form of communication the deeper the relationship will be. When my first marriage was ending and I was living in the back of my van, my only companion was my dog. I came to depend on his presence much the same way, I suppose, he depended on me for sustenance. Without that animal my loneliness would have been unbearable.

I learned different ways to communicate through my animals. I go through life now looking for nonverbal ways to communicate with my grandchildren and my animals. I find that my dogs and horses understand when I'm talking to them, even if they have no idea what my words mean. We are communicating in a different language. That language can be physical; a simple touch can convey extraordinary meaning. Sometimes, for example, I will put my forehead against my dog's forehead and we'll stay that way for a time. Maybe I'm transferring thoughts; I don't know. But on some level we are making a connection. The same thing is true with my horses. There are places on a horse that when touched send a message: Move away. Come close. I love you. You're my friend.

I did not have any pets as a child; my

memory is that my mother believed they made the house too dirty. But as soon as I was on my own and in a position to take care of an animal I did so. One of the most painful moments during my first marriage came over a dog. Our marriage was already shaky when she told me, "I can't take the clicking of the dog's nails on the linoleum floor." It became such an issue that I had to get rid of my dog. It was incredibly difficult. I gave him to a loving veterinarian. I would visit the dog every so often, and I sobbed each time I left. That was the last dog I ever gave up.

Any doubt I had about the ability of a person and an animal to form a relationship ended for me one rainy night in New York City. I was walking my Doberman — long ago I fell in love with that breed, so all my dogs have been Dobermans — one rainy night in New York City. I made the mistake of taking him off the leash briefly to allow him to do his business. For some reason he got spooked and ran between two parked cars. A cab almost hit him, but the driver slammed on the brakes and barely touched him. The dog panicked, he ran back to the building, and, when he couldn't get inside, took off down Lexington Avenue. I ran after him but couldn't keep up. I got into a cab and we went hunting for him. I was desperate. All I could think about was this frightened animal alone in New York. And it was my fault.

We couldn't find the dog. We went from 73rd Street to about 50th Street. I got out of the cab to continue my search on foot. As I walked along shouting his name I noticed a bar directly across the street, but you had to walk down steps to go inside. I went down those stairs; don't ask me why. I looked around the bar and obviously my dog was not there. But I asked the bartender if he had seen a big dog. I was stunned when he nodded and told me, "A dog just ran in here and is cowering in the back room." There he was. My dog, shivering from fear. There was no reason for me to have gone into that bar — or perhaps there was.

I learned so much about relationships from my animals, my horses as well as my dogs. Training an animal is far more simplistic than raising a child — but there are similarities. Stop! I am not in any way comparing children and animals, but your actions can shape both, just as my parents molded me. In both instances the application of love will make the difference. With that come trust and responsibility and pride and almost an endless array of emotions. But the end result will be a relationship from which you can draw great pleasure.

My children's mother and I divorced when they were still young. I became a weekend father. It occurred to me then that in some ways I was repeating the behavior I had learned from my own father. I was the provider, going out to fight the dragon and bringing home food for them, but I was emotionally distant. I was so tired from working to support them that I had little time to be with them. I tried to change that; I tried to take them somewhere every weekend, whether it was riding ponies or on a trip, whatever I could do to amuse and amaze them.

It must have worked to some degree, because they learned to take me for granted. I'm not sure that I accepted it at the time, but that was a very good thing. They knew I was going to be there for them, even if I wasn't living at home with them. What made it difficult for me was that I had all of this wisdom I wanted to share with them; I had knowledge and experiences that I wanted to impart to them; they were far more interested in playing with their friends. I had to learn how to hold myself back; I wanted to say to them, "Listen to me. I've got something important to tell you," but instead I learned how to parcel it out. You have to do it slowly, meal by meal, whether it is a banquet or fast food. You have to take advantage of every opportunity and not force it on anyone. While to me my experience may seem like the most important piece of advice anyone has ever given, to a young person it probably is less important than the last text from a friend about who's hanging at the mall. I had to learn not to take myself, or my profound wisdom, too seriously.

As I have now become certain from both my own experience and those of so many other people, there is no magic formula for raising children beyond doing the best you can and making sure they know you love them. And don't beat yourself up if it isn't perfect. It isn't going to be perfect. Just as every person is unique, so every relationship is unique. Whatever I did, whatever their mother did, it worked, and even with the tension between their mother and myself I have managed to maintain a loving relationship with my daughters.

Even better, having finally learned how to open myself, at least partially, to relationships, I have established loving relationships with my grandchildren. I am now convinced that the most wonderful thing a grandparent can do is hold his grandchild tightly, then hand the child back to his or her parents and tell them, "Here, it's yours." Then go to a movie.

Grandparents frequently have more time available to spend with their grandchildren than they did with their children. It's just a reality of life. And with that time hopefully comes a depth of understanding from both parties. It's never deep enough or often enough for me, but I accept what I can get.

For someone who once couldn't wait to get out of my house to escape into the world, I have come to do as much as I can to bring my family close together. In 2016, I had bracelets made for all fourteen members of my family. These bracelets have the Maori love signs and inside is written "Love is forever." I wear mine all the time. I noticed one day that my granddaughter Natasha wasn't wearing hers and I asked her where it was; she said, "It is the most precious thing that I have, so I put it away. I don't want to lose it."

"You have to wear it," I told her. My family has become my buffer not only against the world but also against my own demons.

In the entire range of relationships, my experience has been that the most difficult of all is living with someone, whether you are married to that person or not. It is fascinating; that kind of close relationship is what living things most crave, someone to be with. I remember walking into my yard one day and seeing two snails out of their shells, shivering from passion as they entwined themselves. Snails. And yet actually sharing your life with someone is fraught with problems.

On occasion I have had young people ask for my advice about marriage; my advice is even more emphatic about that than most other things. My advice is pay no attention to my advice. But what I do know about it may well be the secret to any kind of successful relationship: To form a meaningful relationship with another person you really have to understand him or her — but even more importantly you have to understand yourself.

Understand yourself. Be honest with yourself. Why did I do that? What need was I trying to satisfy? What didn't I understand or comprehend? That is among the hardest things any of us can do. We all have our guises that we present to the world, telling people, This is me. But most of the time it isn't; it's the person you want the world to believe you are. Getting naked in front of another person physically can be difficult; exposing your emotions is far more difficult. But for a marriage or that type of committed relationship to work it is an absolute necessity.

When I look back on my life I realize how protective of my emotions I tried to be. And how that made it difficult for me to have close relationships of any type. At my age I know, I absolutely know, I am a better actor than I have ever been in my life. I know I ride a horse as well as or better than I ever have. And I also know I am far more capable at eighty-seven years old of being part of good relationships than ever before.

Elizabeth, obviously, has contributed greatly to my understanding and acceptance of that. Perhaps I simply was ready for someone like her to come into my life, having been through so much drama in my earlier marriages, but both Elizabeth and I were able to accept each other for who we are, with all we brought to the marriage. The result has been a deeply satisfying relationship on all the important levels.

Oddly enough, it was David Rockefeller, one of the wealthiest people in the world, who once said quite accurately, "I am convinced that material things can contribute a lot to making one's life pleasant, but, basically, if you do not have very good friends and relatives who matter to you, life will be really empty and sad and material things cease to be important."

This was a lesson I have spent my entire life learning.

9.
MY PRINCIPAL BELIEFS

In my career I have played several unusual philosophers: Captain James T. Kirk was continually confronted by the mechanisms of the endlessly fascinating universe gone awry, forcing him to put things right — without imposing Earth's moral code on other civilizations; Police Sergeant T. J. Hooker had seen the dark side of mankind and harbored few illusions about appealing to man's better angels; instead he took the world as it hit him in the face and responded to it bluntly and immediately; Denny Crane was continuously amazed to discover the world did not exist to satisfy his needs, although he did everything possible to correct that error.

I have found that it's easy to have a philosophy of life when you have good writers. But figuring out for yourself the moral principles on which to live your life is a lot more difficult. The basics appear to be easy:

Try to do good deeds. Try not to hurt other people. Be honest. Who could disagree with nice things like that? For me, life has always been a work in progress. It continues to surprise me that at my age things continue to surprise me. I like to believe that at this point I might be able to predict with certainty my own behavior in a situation, and while that is true in most instances I am not always right. It has been my experience that, depending on the situation, I may end up compromising on my most deeply held principles.

We all tend to believe the adage, often misattributed to Alexander Hamilton, "If you don't stand for something, you'll fall for anything." So we follow some often vague set of principles, a morality that we have picked up from those people who most influence us. Eventually we become invested in those beliefs, and feel they are the only moral ones, and have difficulty understanding why someone might believe the opposite of what we do.

The difficulty throughout my life, I've found, is that other people's principles, needs, desires, and reality often conflict with my own beliefs. Sometimes it can't be helped; I try very hard to go through life without hurting other people. But at times when I was working on a series I was handed a less than acceptable script. Being honest means hurting the writer, maybe even costing him the job. On *Star Trek* it meant fighting with the producer. Whatever decision I make means violating one of my principles. Like most people, I try to leave a lot more good in my wake than bad.

Like everyone else, I have not always been successful. There are people who have felt wounded by my actions. I think it might be close to impossible to make your way through the world for eighty-seven years without causing some anger and bitterness. There are times when my needs conflicted with the needs of other people. My first wife, for example, remained angry at me for slights real and imagined for decades. And, honestly, I have held on to my own anger. Several members of the *Star Trek* cast have never forgiven me for things I didn't even know I had done. I understand and accept the fact that people can see the same actions and reach very different conclusions about their meaning. But I can't remember a time when I set out to hurt someone, when my objective was to cause harm to someone. I can state without hesitation that I have always been true to my principles, whatever they were at the time.

One of the more interesting aspects of my profession is that for a brief time I have had the opportunity to test a great variety of different moral structures. Many actors believe playing a role requires you to become that character for a period of time. I don't think I ever inhabited a character that completely, but when creating a life on film or onstage I did have to think through all the moral implications of that person. I had to make certain there was a moral consistency to make the character come to life; bad guys didn't have to wear black hats.

It has not been quite as simple in my own life. Obviously, I have respected and followed the basic moral principles of our society. One of my grandchildren was caught stealing a minor item. It wasn't its value that bothered us, rather the act of stealing. This is the basic right and wrong. Although her parents handled it, I happened to get involved. I told her, "Lying and stealing is going to destroy you."

Essentially what I was saying to her is that this is what I believe, based on my own experiences: On the one hand, you may become Bernie Madoff and be the best thief we have seen; on the other hand, Bernie Madoff is in jail and perhaps wishes he were dead. Don't lie; don't cheat; don't steal. Try to do good things, don't hurt living beings; other than that, the rest is up to you.

One thing I know to be true about my life is that I am a very different person today than I have been at various times of my life. Those things that once seemed essential no longer are very important. Many of my beliefs have changed; even some of my principles have changed. Whether out of choice or necessity, I have embraced change, and my life has been the better for it.

It seems to me that many of us fight an endless battle between ethics and principles. I have heard many people say that they live by their principles and those principles are unchangeable. There is right and there is wrong and they know the difference. They know who they are, what they believe, and these are the guiding stars of their life. They sometimes refer to it as honor; living by their principles is a matter of honor. I understand that. Before a show opens on Broadway there is extensive rehearsal. Every line, every moment, is practiced. Whether you hang your coat on the back of a chair or toss it on a couch is determined by the director, and whatever the direction, it can't change every night. One slight change might throw the entire performance out of whack. In theory that show is going to be exactly the same every performance as it was on opening night. But the reality is quite different. Live theater is not a movie; in subtle ways every performance is different. If, for example, you put down a glass of water three inches to the right of where it is supposed to be, over time that three inches will become a foot. Tiny things change and accumulate and eventually the change becomes massive. Or you change slightly the inflection of a line and a question becomes a statement and suddenly the audience doesn't understand the important information the playwright wanted them to have. Every actor on that stage has to be cognizant of every small change, so either you correct it or all your fellow actors are forced to adjust to it. I've found that life is like that.

On the one hand, if you "freeze your life" you have maintained your principles: "This is what I believe under all conditions." On the other hand, you haven't adjusted to all the changes taking place around you. This is where principles and compromise conflict.

At times all of us have heard people say, "These are my principles," with an upraised index finger emphasizing their authoritarian demeanor. Classically we romanticize the person who sticks to his or her principles and refuses to compromise. Of course, as Sir Thomas More learned, the result of that might be that they cut off your head. Thomas More made his point, but so did Henry VIII, although the king made his a bit more emphatically.

I've seen that in acting. Actors often defend their choices. One of the most memorable skits from the early days of *Saturday Night Live* was called "The Coneheads." They were aliens with heads that came to a cone top. It was very broad comedy. They were intentionally absurd in their efforts to figure out society. Supposedly, after the skit had become popular the actors were doing a table reading of a sketch and one of the actors balked at a suggested action, explaining firmly, "Oh no, the Coneheads wouldn't do that." Who knew these aliens with coneheads had irrevocable principles?

I guess that is as good a way as any of describing an inability to compromise: The Coneheads wouldn't do that. This is a frequent problem in my profession: The director says, "I have a vision and this is what I need you to do to help me fulfill my vision." In response the actor says, "I understand my character far better than you do, as I have created it, and my character would never do that. It is inconsistent with everything he [or she] is." Creating a character means that he must be the same person in June as he was in January, although the director wasn't there in January, so he doesn't know that. Having been both an actor and a director, I have been on both sides of that particular equation.

Tell me how to forge a compromise in that situation. And that's when there is only a performance at stake. Real life is a lot more complex and the consequences are far greater. There was a wonderful book written about Israeli paratroopers, the 55th Paratrooper Brigade, known as Israel's "tip of the spear." These are among the most elite soldiers in the world. Yet at one point Israeli security discovered a member of that elite group colluding with the Palestinians. He took these actions, he explained after being caught, based on his principles. He believed creating a two-state solution was the path to peace and his actions were furthering those beliefs. He was willing to give up his freedom and, if necessary, his life for his principles. Even though those principles might put the lives of his fellow soldiers in jeopardy, he refused to compromise.

I understand that reasoning. I don't agree

with it, but I do understand it. I think we have seen the results of that thinking in recent American politics. The only thing on which everyone can agree is that both sides have stuck to their political principles and as a result very little has gotten accomplished. In my life I have seen the benefits of compromise, a solution in which everyone gets at least part of what they need. Why would you go to jail for a principle? At my age I have learned to treat every day with the level of preciousness that my grandchildren should embrace. Every day of your life is precious. To see the sky, breathe the air, walk along and feel your body is precious because our days are numbered. There are people who are willing to do this, people willing to stand up for a principle and go to jail for years and refuse to give up. What is more precious: freedom or your principles? Each person has to answer that themselves.

There are exceptions to that, of course. Many people believe Jesus Christ gave his mortal life as a lesson to them. To me, the most extraordinary example in my lifetime has been Nelson Mandela, who was willing to go to jail for most of his life to protest legalized inhuman treatment by the government of South Africa. How can anyone not admire someone like that? He was an amazing man whose refusal to compromise literally changed the world. I feel the same way about soldiers who fight when their country is threatened. We are clannish by nature; we protect our cave, our clan, our tribe, and our country. We send our young people out to protect our clan. If the Nazis are encroaching on your country, you have to fight. If the government is treating you as a slave, you have to fight. If the fascist state is going to kill your family, you have to fight. I can see myself doing that, standing in front of my family to protect them from an oppressor. Ethics change and it is absurd not to acknowledge that: Thou shalt not kill, but the truth is that thou shall kill under certain circumstances.

Obviously there are some principles worth fighting and dying for, but that is at the extreme end and most people won't encounter that situation. The things we have to deal with generally are much more personal and considerably less important. One day in 2015 I was driving on Ventura Boulevard and I had to make a left turn. I probably cut in front of someone to do that, because he responded by getting very close and honking his horn. A lot. That was his space and I had invaded it. He was doing the right thing and I had done the wrong thing, and he was standing up for his principle. I made my left, believing that would be the end of it, but he made a left, too. I sped up and he stayed with me, and we were racing down the road. I went around a truck, thinking he could be cut off, and he made an expert move and went around the truck and cut in front of me. I slammed on my brakes. A young man practically leaped out of that car and started walking toward me. I got out of my car and started walking toward him, my fists clenched. To do what? If we got into a fight it would take him one punch to beat me to a pulp. But I was ready to fight. I wasn't going to back down. This thing had escalated from a silly move on my part into a potentially dangerous situation. Neither one of us appeared willing to back down. We had our honor to defend. Our principles! Then he said, "William Shatner. I used to stunt for you." He was a professional stuntman and we had worked together. We both started laughing at the absurdity of the situation.

For Jews, living up to your principles has too often meant dying for them. During the Spanish Inquisition, Jews were given a choice: renounce your religion or die. My answer would have been simple: "I have been Catholic my entire life. I believe in Jesus and Jesus saves me." Prior to and even during World War II admitting to being a Jew often was a prelude to a death sentence and countless Jews lived as Christians rather than dying as Jews.

Of course we tend to admire those people who sacrificed their lives for their principles. But dying to prove to other people that holding on to your principles is more important than life itself seems self-defeating. Living and spreading those principles seems to me to be more effective. Joan of Arc was burned at the stake for refusing to compromise on her principles. Sir Thomas More, as I wrote, had his head cut off for refusing to compromise on his principles. These people live in our history for dying. But what is more important, saving your life to perhaps fight another day or dying for your ethics and principles? I don't know if I am right or wrong for anyone else here, but I do know how I feel about it.

Why couldn't they have compromised? Why couldn't Joan of Arc have said, "I have a split personality; I am bipolar," and after her jailers left said, "I am not bipolar. I only said that to live"? Why couldn't you renounce your Judaism to the Inquisitors and when the Inquisition was done go to synagogue or daven in the basement? The German-Jewish philosopher Martin Buber stood up to the Nazis when they began passing anti-Jewish regulations, certainly risking his life. But when he understood the consequences of his actions he accepted a compromise, leaving his beloved Germany and immigrating to then-Palestine in 1938. What is the principle that allows only obeisance without any room for compromise? That mystery eludes me and fascinates me. When I think about it, if I were in that circumstance can I say without any doubt what I would have done? It is impossible to have been born Jewish before World War II and not think about what you would have done if you were trapped in Europe. I like to believe I would have found a way to survive. I like to believe I would have done whatever was necessary to survive.

What type of personality requires an uncompromising stand on principle? It would have to be someone who was completely rigid, completely inflexible, and often has some sort of megalomania: I believe this is the only truth, and it is the only truth because I believe it.

My experience has been that almost always there is a third way of doing things, and that third way, the compromise, in my experience often turns out to be better than either side. There are many ways to say a line or lead your life, but there is only one way to stand on principle. I suspect one reason religion has not played a significant role in my adult life is because I tend to stray far away from any type of prescribed orthodoxy, anything that tells you, This is the path to follow and if you don't follow it you're going to burn for all eternity, or at least have to do some penance. As I wrote chapters ago, we are all different, we are all unique; the reason I have hesitated to give any advice is because I don't have the slightest idea if it is right or wrong for anyone else. The only principle that has worked for me in my lifetime is don't be too rigid about your principles. Don't make claims about right and wrong, about what you will do or not do. Too often we end up in conflict with someone whose principles are the opposite of ours. Those are the moments when you hope the other person isn't armed. And when you finally realize you have to reach some sort of compromise. There are a lot of expressions used to describe this situation: backing down, selling out, all derogatory terms that infer you did something wrong. I have a friend who used humor to get out of situations like this. When faced with the possibility of a fight he would stand up straight and tell the other person, "There are only two things that can happen if we fight. Either I'm going to get hurt, or I'm going to get very badly hurt." That always diffused the situation.

Life is a continuous series of compromises. Many of them are easy: We won't go to Santa Barbara; we'll go to Rancho Santa Fe. I'll cut back on sugar, but I'm still going to have dessert. There are life-changing decisions that have to be made every day. I have seen that over and over: Should you take that teaching job you were offered or wait on tables and do the other low-wage jobs that leave you free to go to auditions at eleven o'clock in the morning. Should you take the character part that means you'll be a bad guy or the third person through the door when you believe in your own heroic capabilities? Martin Buber understood that, writing: "I do not accept any absolute formulas for living. No preconceived code can see ahead to everything that can happen in a man's life. As we live, we grow and our beliefs change. They must change. So I think we should live with this constant discovery. We should be open to this adventure in heightened awareness of living. We should stake our whole existence on our willingness to explore and experience."

The difficulty is figuring out when to make those compromises. When do you stand on principle and when do you compromise? When do you refuse to stand for the National Anthem like former San Francisco 49ers quarterback Colin Kaepernick and when do you stand up tall? When do you turn down a job offer, end a relationship, walk away? The answer for each of us is different and it often is very difficult to make that decision.

Compromising doesn't guarantee anything other than neither side gets everything they want. Sometimes that works out; compromise can be a negotiating tool — when negotiating a contract, for example, more often you end up at a compromise figure than what you originally wanted. But other times compromising turns out to be the wrong decision. Acting and directing are collaborative efforts and by nature require compromise. When I was directing a *Star Trek* movie, for example, I had this wonderful concept about the *Enterprise* searching for God but finding the devil. Imagine, the crew fighting its way out of hell! The possibilities were mind-boggling, and my mind was appropriately boggled with ideas. Then producer Gene Rodenberry turned it down.

It was potentially too divisive, he said; too many people might object. We eventually compromised; rather than the true devil, the crew encountered an alien who believed he was the devil.

I had a choice: I could accept the compromise or refuse to direct the movie. I made a mistake; I accepted the compromise, which doomed the picture from the beginning.

I have made decisions, many decisions, in my life that I would change knowing what I now know. But at that time I didn't know it and I made the best possible decision for me, the one I could live with. In retrospect, it may not have been the best decision, but it was consistent with who I was at the time. I desperately wanted to direct that picture, for example, and was willing to accept the compromise to get what I wanted. I made the right decision for me at the time, I was willing to be flexible with my principles, but the results proved it was the wrong decision.

I suspect we all like to think we are in most ways the same person throughout our lifetimes. Well, I am here to tell you we are not. Anyone who claims to have the same principles at my age as they had in their twenties simply hasn't learned anything from their experiences. I have changed many times in my lifetime. We accept physical changes out of necessity: As you get older your feet hurt, your legs hurt, and your shoulder hurts. I love skiing, I love to ski as much as I love riding horses, but I accept the fact that I no longer have the legs to ski. My body doesn't bend as it used to; my legs aren't as strong. If I fall I will have difficulty getting up. The same thing is true about staying up all night drinking and then showing up for work the next morning. At a certain point your body tells you don't do it, so you change your behaviors. I try to limit the change because I don't want to give in to the ills of aging, but I recognize and accept the necessity of making physical changes.

I also have seen changes in my morals. It amazes and appalls me that I once celebrated the hunt for a wild beast. I found nothing wrong with hunting down and killing beautiful animals and I did so without the slightest hesitation. I did it for sport; I did it with TV crews watching my prowess with a bow and arrow. Who was that person? I now wonder. When did I change? What caused that change? And that clearly was only one of many changes I've made as I've gotten older and gathered knowledge and experience. What happened to holding on to those principles in which I once so fervently believed?

You can't really believe in the sanctity of life while killing living creatures. I have little objection to friends' hunting and eating what they kill. That is their decision. But I now find myself giving up eating meat for a variety of reasons, including philosophical. Perhaps as a function of age I have come to place a greater value on all life than I did years ago. Perhaps.

A lot of people resist change. They figure, This has always worked for me so why should I change? They think, I've made a lot of money doing things my way, so why should I change? I don't have an answer for them; maybe they're right. If that philosophy continues to work for them, who am I to tell anyone else they are right or wrong? Change for the sake of change can be dangerous and we don't know where it might lead. The Constitution of the United States was written more than two centuries ago. Strict constitutionalists don't want to change it at all. On the one hand, I understand there is good reason not to change it. People would prefer to hold tight to those precepts written in stone. If we don't stick to the Constitution then gradually it will erode and eventually those principles on which this country was founded will be lost. On the other hand, throughout history any civilization that has refused to evolve to meet changing reality has disappeared. There are many people who feel the principles enumerated in that document are inviolate and it is those broad principles rather than the enumerated amendments that need to be defended. Of course, we have already fought the bloodiest war in American history over those same principles.

My interview show, *Raw Nerve,* gave me the opportunity to explore concepts like this with a lot of smart, successful people. What I found was that two people, both of whom clearly are intelligent, could subscribe to totally different philosophies and principles and be equally convinced they are absolutely correct and, in fact, believe without reservation that these are the only valid principles. I had conservative radio broadcaster Rush Limbaugh as my guest; whatever you might think about him, he is well informed and smart. During our conversation he compared having health care to owning a home, telling me, "You're assuming that there's some morally superior aspect to health care than there is to a house. . . ." Actually, I was. And while his beliefs conflicted with

232

my principles, he explained he felt that way because "it's my job; it's my life; it's my career; it's my passion. I've studied this stuff. I want the best country we can have, and this is not the way to get it."

Sometime later I invited him to my home for one of my *Monday Night Football* parties. I have a wall-sized television and host a gathering for several of those games. In addition to Limbaugh I had an extremely liberal friend there that night. Both of them smart people, and their principles, their political beliefs at least, could not be further apart. During the evening I watched my liberal friend, who obviously knew who Limbaugh was, artfully avoid any contact with him at all. My liberal friend sat on the other side of the room; when Limbaugh came to his side he buried his head in the refrigerator. He had no interest in even being introduced to Limbaugh. What occurred to me, as I watched this play out, was how invested each of us becomes in our beliefs and principles. And how quickly we judge people based on their beliefs.

I don't think any of my other guests were aware of this playing out. Was my liberal friend right? Was he wrong? Did he miss an opportunity? I'm certain Limbaugh never even realized this was taking place.

An important lesson I have learned, and it took me a long time to learn it, is the danger of being judgmental. It serves no purpose. I support the people and causes in which I believe and try not to say too much about those things with which I disagree. But I do believe there is at least one truth that is the sum total of my experiences. I had been to South Africa several times, but I had never been to the townships, the black villages that had been established during apartheid. When I was filming in that country in 2017, I said I wanted to visit one of them. It wasn't a good idea, I was told; it was too dangerous. But I insisted. I was accompanied by a well-armed guard. What I saw there was quite different than I anticipated. I saw fathers playing with children. I saw teenagers playing ball with one another. I saw young girls in school uniforms walking hand in hand. I saw their small shacks, each of which had a television and a satellite dish. I had seen this degree of poverty before, but I had never felt the level of peacefulness I found in that township. When we drove by they looked at us with curiosity but not hostility. I did not sense the danger I had been warned about. These were people living closely together — in harmony.

It surprised me. I started talking about

this with my driver. "Yes," he said, "what you are feeling is called *ubuntu*. It is a Zulu word meaning, generally, you are not a human being until you express your humanity with other human beings." My guide, my guard, gave me an example: "It means how can you be happy when a child is starving?"

There is no English equivalent to that word. Essentially, I came to understand, it simply means real happiness comes from helping other people. There was a time in America when neighbors helped their neighbors, but the reality is that now too often we don't even know our neighbors beyond a nodding recognition. Nobody has a barn-raising anymore. In a time when social media makes us readily available to almost anyone on earth, many of us are isolated. It reminded me of something I had realized after Leonard Nimoy's death. It was made clear to me that I was not welcome at his funeral. That was painful. I had an easy excuse. Months earlier I had agreed to appear at a Red Cross fund-raiser being held by Donald Trump at Mar-a-Lago that same day. Millions of dollars had been raised. The media, naturally, made a big deal of the fact that I did not attend the funeral. At that dinner I told the guests, "I want all of us to remember the name Leonard Nimoy as long as we can, but I know that within a few years his name will be forgotten. Over time all of the great movie stars, all of our leaders, all of us, will be forgotten. There might be a statue or a building named after that person, but people will wonder who it was.

"But the good deeds we are doing here tonight may well reverberate until the end of time. That child that you are helping keep alive by being here tonight will go on to live his or her life and eventually have children who will have children. While you may not even think being here tonight is a good deed, it may well justify your existence until the end of time."

I believe that without reservation. My father was very active in charitable organizations in Montreal. He used some of the money he was able to save to bring other members of his family from Europe to Canada and America. He changed lives forever. And he lives on in me. So as I said that night, long after my name has been forgotten the good deeds that I did will continue to live on through other people.

It is odd, those things we remember late in life. Those events that happened early in our lives that continue to have an impact as long as we live. At the beginning of my career I accepted an invitation to join

Tyrone Guthrie's Stratford Festival. I packed all my possessions into a used Morris Minor, a very small car that my father had loaned me $400 to purchase, and headed toward Toronto. During a torrential rainstorm I was crossing a rickety bridge while a massive sixteen-wheeler was coming from the other direction. As we got closer the air this truck was displacing pushed my little car to the side and for an instant I thought I was going off the bridge. That instant of fear, whether or not it was rational, has lived inside me for the rest of my life. It wasn't so much the possibility of dying but rather the realization that if I had been killed on that bridge, nobody but my parents would mourn for me. It would be as if I had not existed in this world. I wouldn't have left a scratch on the world to prove that I had been here, even for a brief period of time. That's what really terrified me. And that feeling has never gone away. This need to justify my existence in this world has been a motivating factor in my life.

And after living all my years, after all I have seen and done and learned, after sorting through an array of principles and personal ethics, I have come to believe that making that mark, that leaving behind some

slight evidence that proved you were here,
matters most of all.

10.
Where Does Time Go?

Where does time go:
I finish the dishes, I go to the store; before I
  know it, time is no more.
I plan for the weekend, I drive to the sea,
  stop for lunch at the deli, no time for tea.
Where does time go: Into space that it flies,
  a power that takes it, and no one ask
  why, or where it lies,
With only you is there peace and
  everything slows down, at last my mind
  rests and all is profound.
I need you beside me to push back the
  past. With us holding each other, we can
  make time last.
Where does time go: For dreams for each
  other we can make the time last, we can
  make the time last.
In time, the earth disappears, along with
  our hopes and dreams and fears, all of
  history gone in a cloud.
Nothing remains; ambition, empires,

> soldiers so proud, where does time go
> when it comes to an end?
> All that is us with time we will blend.

Those are the lyrics to a song I wrote with Billy Sherwood titled, properly, "Where Does Time Go." It is, obviously, about the most profound mystery of life: death. Believe me, as I have gotten older I have thought about it, I have wondered about it, I have had nightmares about it. In a weird way, I can't bring myself to believe that I am going to die.

Every person I have ever known, everything I have ever read, at some point ponders the mystery of life and death. The most ignorant people in history still looked up into the night sky and wondered, What the heck is that? There were people who believed the stars were simply tricks with light. All the attempts to explain it eventually evolved into what we now call religion. And as an inducement to follow a certain religion people were offered the one thing they craved: eternal life, in one form or another.

My first real contact with death was my father's sudden death. I took it very hard and grieved for more than a year. Until then I hadn't been forced to confront death. I was aware of the Holocaust, and I was told relatives of mine in Europe had been put to death, but I didn't know them, so they remained remote. They didn't touch me. After my father died I spent a considerable length of time trying to understand this thing, death, and eventually came to the realization there is no way to understand it. Since then, I have seen many loved ones die. The pain of their loss becomes part of my life. The drowning death of my wife Nerine haunts me. I found her in our pool and lifted her out of the water. The emergency responders rushed to the house, but there was nothing that could be done. I saw her body lying there in the moonlight. She was as beautiful then as she had been in life, but everything about her was gone. Her voice, her laughter, her pleasures, and her fears. Everything that made her the person she was — with the exception of a physical presence — was gone.

I have held tight to several beloved animals as they died. I have looked in their eyes as the life force went out of them. My beloved Starbuck lived to fifteen, a great age for a Doberman. I wrote a lyric for him, "His muzzle is gray, his back is sore and he is a little cloudy of eye; Then the truth of what I see is so am I? . . . Now he is old and stiff and sore and getting ready to die. I look at him with love and realize, so am I." I had a champion stallion who was suffering terribly. He was about to be put down by the veterinarians. We dug a grave for him and led him to it. As we did, a younger horse came to the fence to watch. The stallion, in a final act of noble defiance, reared up on his bandaged legs and neighed, frightening away the other horses. Seconds after the veterinarian gave him the drug he collapsed into the hole. The life force that had been in him seconds before was gone. It is unimaginable. I can't understand, no one can understand, what that force is. In one second there is this energy, life, intelligence, and glamour, there is knowledge and history; and in the next second you are in the earth, as dead as the soil in which you are buried. It happens in an instant. What is that magical thing that made the difference between Starbuck being alive on the kitchen floor and seconds later dead in my arms? What is that? What is that miracle that fires your engine? We don't know what that life force is. What is it that makes the cells cease to function? We think it might be amino acids, but it might just as easily be sunlight or thunder for all we know. That is what has been worshipped as long as rational mankind has existed.

The playwright Robert Anderson wrote so accurately in *I Never Sang for My Father*: "Death ends a life, but it does not end a relationship, which struggles on in the survivor's mind toward some final resolution, some clear meaning, which it perhaps never finds." But the one thing that the death of a loved one or even a beloved pet does not prepare you for is your own death.

I find it very difficult to grasp the reality that I am going to die. Many other people around me have died. But me? It seems impossible that all of this that I have built around me will no longer have any meaning to me. The entire concept of some form of life after death exists because the concept of a final ending is beyond anything we can comprehend. That's one reason we appreciate spirit and ghost stories, as those exist as a form between the life we live on Earth and whatever it is that comes next. That's a reason so many of us respond to stories of out-of-body experiences or people coming back from "the light." They at least hint at the possibility there is more than this life.

I've wondered about that; I've wondered about it a lot. Where does that life force go? What happens to it? It is matter, and the greatest minds tell us matter cannot be made or lost. So that life force cannot possibly be lost into the universe of inanimate matter. But where does it go? What form does it take?

As far as the afterlife proposed by religions, I don't believe there is any form of pearly gates waiting to welcome me, nor do I believe there is a horned creature with a pitchfork inviting me to spend eternity with him. I wish I did. But it defies logic. When I meet my parents, will they be their younger selves and I won't recognize them? I have been married several times; which wife do I spend eternity with? What about the people I've fought with? Will they be there and finally realize I was right?

So I don't accept the vision of angels with wings and an unlimited buffet, although I am heartened by the possibilities. It is absurd to believe we know the answer. We know so little about our world. We don't have a clue how matter was formed, or why. It is obviously beyond our tiny imaginations at this point. During a discussion about the possibility of a Divine presence we were having, a friend of mine quoted a phrase: "The eyes cannot see what the mind cannot encompass."

I responded, "What about discovery?" Discovering something means it wasn't known before you discovered it. There is a legend that claims when Columbus's ships sailed to the Americas the Indians didn't see his ships because they couldn't imagine such things existed. Applying that to the concept of a Divine Being doesn't make sense to me. That within the minutia of our logic a being is watching over the billions of our lives?

Conversely, there have been so many fortuitous events in my life that sometimes it is difficult to believe there is not some greater plan.

I want to believe there is more to come. From that night as a camper when I was completely overwhelmed by the vastness of the universe, I have never lost my awe for the majesty of creation. We have no idea what's out there; on a regular basis astrophysicists discover things they can't explain. Why is the universe expanding rather than contracting? What is light? What is a photon of light? I can spout these terms, but I don't know what they mean. Even those things we now believe in many cases will be modified: We know with great certainty the speed of light and that will never change, but who knows?

The fact that we know so little encourages me. It is my feeling that without question there are multiple life-forms, far more than we now comprehend. I don't mean Klingons, but I have seen that forms of life have filled every available niche. Scientists have found unique life forms able to survive at seven hundred degrees at the bottoms of the oceans and under the ice in the Arctic cold. Life is energetic and prolific. There is so much we can't explain in scientific terms right in front of us that the possibility that there is more to existence can't be ignored.

But death, as we understand it, is the ultimate stop sign. It means you can go no further along this road. There is no exit; there isn't even a roundabout. I fear it. Whatever else there might be, this beautiful present will be gone, and I am loving every second I can hold on to my life. The fact that I will no longer be has great tragic overtones to me. I will never see my wife and my children, all of the wonderful things that are part of my life, again. In 2017, two of my dogs whom I loved so dearly died. It seemed to me they were just pups and then they became limp bodies that I buried in my backyard. They were here, and then gone forever. I am frightened practically to death by the inevitability of death.

There are many people who find solace in their religion. I envy my religious friends who believe in the afterlife. I have seen that people who believe in their ideology with the totality of their being, with absolute faith, without skepticism, embrace the possibility of death because they accept without doubt that this is just a beginning. It is simply, if you truly believe, your religion allows you to accept unanswerable questions. It provides some semblance of peace in the face of great tragedy. In fact, for that true believer, their faith does give them most of what they expect from it. I remember when Liz's mother died, Liz went to the hospital. While she was there a woman came up to her and said, "I deal in life-ending care at a hospice. And I can tell you that right now your grandmother is hovering over you." In an odd way, that provided great comfort for Liz at a terrible time.

A member of my family became a born-again Christian. I didn't understand it. She had graduated from a fine university and was a very intelligent person. Yet she was teaching her children that the earth was five thousand years old, that the Bible is literally the word of God, and that human beings emerged as we are today rather than having evolved. I tried to talk to her; I asked if it was possible that evolution was the way God worked. But she was not in a place to listen. That was difficult for me, but she had found a certain peace by giving herself over to that. She had found a form that answered all her questions and fulfilled her needs and fears.

I can't go there. I can't believe that after death there is some form of life similar to what we are living. Logic suggests that our energy, our matter, assumes another shape. That makes the most sense to me, although it lacks the level of grandeur that the universe has shown to us. I would love to explain the mysteries of the world by referring to the hand of God, but there is nothing that comforting for me out there, that the amazing things that have happened to me in my life have been the result of Divine Intervention, but I am stuck with the belief that any answers will be found in science, in the laws of quantum physics that we haven't yet begun to understand.

To me, the essence of religion is the respect it pays to nature and the mysteries of the universe. If you light a candle and say a prayer you are respecting that mystery. The concept of God is a large one. But I think it refers more to the mystery than the embodiment of a single entity. What I admire most about certain religions is the belief that every human being is unique and needs to be treated with respect. The problem, for me at least, isn't the religions themselves but rather how they are taken over by people who often use them for their own advancement.

In too many instances religion is used to manipulate people, to take from them rather than give to them, as an excuse to further the agenda of people seeking power. It is a cliché, but more wars have been fought in the name of God, a whole variety of Gods, than for any other reason. The hypocrisy in many instances has always amazed me: "We are a peaceful religion fighting wars to bring peace to people who worship a different God." Explain that to me?

I did have the semblance of a religious upbringing. I had a bar mitzvah. My devout Uncle Louie told me if I wore a tefillin, a box containing fragments of the Torah affixed to your arm with leather straps, for a year he would give me a $50 bond. I agreed to try. What I remember most about that was how harsh the leather straps were. The edges cut into my skin and it was exceedingly uncomfortable. I remember wondering why they didn't use deerskin, which was soft, rather than rough leather. I never earned that bond. In fact, if anything, this experience helped break whatever bonds to religion that I might have had. So I haven't found solace by turning to religion. But I am hedging my bets. A friend of mine, who believes as I do, is married to a religious woman. And when he expresses his doubt about an afterlife, she tells him he will regret it: "After you die, when someone says to you —"

He stops her right there. "If I'm dead and someone says anything to me, I'm in!"

What I do believe, based on the little that I know, is that all of us are made of the same elements that comprise the universe. We are all one thing; when I stand outside and consider the vastness of the sky and feel my spirit and my soul, my electrical being going out into the universe, that becomes clear to me. When we disappear we become stardust, and stardust is what coagulates and forms the stars, and that has been going on for billions of years. It is a continuous flux of energy into matter and back into energy and we are part of it. That stardust is us. We are all part of the same thing: Our differences, whether it is our DNA or our chosen religion, are far more alike than they are dissimilar. There is something magical going on. Wise men have felt this for almost the entire history of mankind and been trying to put it into words, and those words eventually evolved into the body of wonder we call religion. While at the same time other great men have been probing and testing and speculating and the body of knowledge they amassed is science.

I look back at all the civilizations that tried to conquer the known world and subject the inhabitants to their rule. That has been a dream throughout recorded history — and in every instance it eventually has faded into nothing. All that vanity, and then it is gone, and then history repeats itself. For a time it seems so complicated, but in fact it is so ridiculous. Nothing lasts. Nothing.

What will that moment be like when I know that I am dying? I stayed with my dogs as they were slowly dying. I was there as life leached out of them as I did my best to comfort them, to try to make them feel better. But I could see death coming to them, as if they were slowly sinking into a bog.

I write this with considerable discomfort: When I die, I hope I don't feel the incredible loneliness, that end-of-the-world, cataclysmic feeling of loneliness. I have felt that, that feeling of nowhere to go, of no one to turn to; it is my hope that when that moment of death comes I don't have time to think about how lonely I will be. What I do hope happens is that I am overwhelmed by a sense of curiosity. That I will have time to wonder: What is this going to be like?

So it appears to me that this life is all there is. I was born into a privileged life. I understand and appreciate that. For me, it is the most joyful voyage possible — but that's not true for everyone. I suspect many people suffering from famine, pestilence, war, disease, extremely painful conditions, people living under harsh dictatorships, people who have no control over their own lives and at times have to watch their children suffer, see death quite differently than I do. For them, death is the end of a torturous journey and ahead of them lies the allure of heaven and life after death. I understand that, but it is not true for me. So I read the medical stories, I exercise, I do whatever I can to stay healthy. I listen to the experts, I go with their flow, changing when it seems logical, doing whatever I can do to keep going. There is, however, one thing I try very hard not to do: allow my fear of death to cause me to lose my passion for living. Until my very last breath I want to be actively engaged in life. I know there are some deeply religious people who can't wait to die because they know they will be welcome in the kingdom of heaven. How unfortunate for them, I think, because the rest of us treasure every minute as our time runs down, while they seem to believe life is a test, keeping them from their true destiny.

Time does go by so very quickly. People measure it in so many different ways. One person I know uses the *Gilligan's Island* scale: A three-hour meeting is six *Gilligan's Island* episodes long. Is it worth it?

This fear of death too often casts a dark shadow over the remaining years of life, however many they are. I rarely ask people about their health, because at my age people will be happy to tell you. Worse, when you're in a group talking about your physical condition people try to top you. "You had your knee replaced? I'll raise you a second knee and a hip!"

Other people may accept death peacefully. Not me — when I go, I'm going kicking and screaming. I'm holding onto the furniture. And until that time on a daily basis I do as much as possible to stay fully engaged with the world. I am working as frequently as I ever have, and I am making plans for my future. I am keeping up with changes in society and technology; I may not be able to program my own computer, but when a new communications tool becomes available, I make a point to learn about it and use it. I am on both Twitter and Facebook on a regular basis; I tweet and post regularly, for example. I am actively involved in social media; I have more than 2.5 million followers on Twitter and another 2 million on Facebook. I use Twitter to raise money for my charities — we had a silent auction for the horse show and tripled the money we'd made in previous years; I also use it to promote my projects and those of friends, to connect with fans and on occasion to get in a bit of a scuffle with a troll or just to make an enjoyable point — as I did one May 5 when I tweeted a photo of a jar of Hellman's mayonnaise in a kitchen sink as a way of wishing everyone a very happy Sinko de Mayo.

I also have begun to get involved with virtual reality. In my lifetime we have gone from black-and-white movies to television to performing holograms and virtual reality. When we were making *Star Trek,* none of us actually believed we might live to see the *Enterprise*'s holodeck become reality; it was special effects and, in those days, the effects weren't very special. We would point our plastic guns, our "phasers," and in the editing room someone would add what appeared to be a beam. That was a special effect. Ironically, within a few years people will be able to interact with "me," or my avatar, on a "holodeck" in their own home.

In early 2017, I had some experts in virtual reality come into my office to begin creating my VR image. They filmed every aspect of my body, even my musculature, everything necessary to enable technicians to make my image move and speak realistically. Now if they can just figure out how to make that image consciously think like me and feel like me and believe it is me then perhaps I might not fear death so much. But because of that image, Shatner will now "live" forever — or at least until the sun burns out and becomes a frozen ice ball racing through space.

Meanwhile, I intend to keep living, thank you very much. To me, among other things living means staying involved on a daily basis with the world. I watch the news stations and, admittedly, find it somewhat humorous to hear people commenting that the world is in terrible shape, the situation is at least as dire as it has ever been. Another of the few advantages of being older is that you have lived through so many historic events. I am a Jew who lived through the Third Reich. I lived through the dropping of atomic weapons on cities. I've lived through the Depression. I've lived through the spread of communism and the erection of the Iron Curtain. I have seen endless brutal dictators take power and disappear. I have seen Hitler and Pol Pot, Stalin and Mao, and the various North Korean dictators. I've seen massacres in wartime Europe, communist countries, Vietnam villages, and American schools. So those events I am witnessing on my TV set and iPad and phone and every other available device certainly don't seem to be any worse than what has taken place in my lifetime. The significant difference, obviously, is that I now can see them as they are happening anywhere in the world and I can watch endless discussions and rehashes and interpretations of what happened. In earlier years the news came to us by horseback, then teletype, then radio and newsreels; now the perpetrators use cameras to record their crimes as a means of spreading fear and propaganda. The world is in sad shape today, but the good news is that the world has always been in sad shape! Being alive means being aware of it all, which I try to do.

I am told that depressed people lose interest in events and people. They often isolate themselves. I wonder if it might be the opposite: People who lose interest in those things, perhaps because they feel death approaching, invite depression into their lives.

It seems to be that is the obvious result of succumbing to the power in their life, I have nothing to live for, syndrome. I have a very simple philosophy I follow: If you can get up, get up. Don't give in to anything.

I never plan for death; rather, I plan for life. People have asked me many times what I would like the inscription on my tombstone to be. And my answer each time is that I don't have the slightest idea, I haven't thought about it — nor do I intend to. I have heard all the jokes and clever inscriptions. I have read that lifetime Dodgers player and manager Tommy Lasorda plans to have an electronic screen on his tombstone with the Dodgers' upcoming schedule. I have laughed at Merv Griffin's inscription, "I will not be right back after this message," and Rodney Dangerfield's "There goes the neighborhood," but it isn't that important to me.

That's about death; I am too busy focusing on life. That's another one of my strategies, although I wouldn't call it that: I would say simply that I am continuing to do what I have always done. In this case that means surrounding myself with young life as much as possible. In addition to the time I spend with my grandkids, which is essentially as much time as they allow me to be around them, Liz and I got a new puppy in early 2017. She is a daughter of Starbuck that we bred through artificial insemination. We currently are setting up a larger breeding program. I want to breed this dog so there continually is new life coming into my orbit. I know older people who refuse to get a new animal because they are afraid it will outlive them. My answer to that is, So what? Animals adapt to the situation.

We continue to breed our horses, too. I've heard it said that you will never find someone who has a mare in foal committing suicide, because the anticipation is too great. Obviously I feel the same way about my dogs. Each birth is the beginning of possibilities. I may see some or all of them come to fruition or I may not; I never think about it, so I never allow that possibility to hold me back. When I watch the puppy or the foal, I share their joy in exploring life, in learning that walls are hard when you run into them and a human hand is not something to be afraid of, and it brings great pleasure to me. I have no concept of what is going to happen in my life in the next few years. People now ask me how it feels to be my age. I respond with the truth: I don't know, I've never been this age before. Actually, that isn't precisely true. Several times in my career I had played myself as a much older man. We did an episode of *Star Trek* in 1967 titled "The Deadly Years," in which the *Enterprise* visited Gamma Hydra IV and the landing party, which included the essential members of the crew, contracted a bizarre condition in which we aged approximately thirty years a day. My explanation for that was simple: "I admit, I'm getting a little gray, but radiation will do that to you." I don't remember much about filming this episode or how I decided to act old. I do know that it took several hours to apply my makeup. Looking at photographs of me taken fifty years ago as I was made up to look about the age I am today, I am somewhat startled at what a good job they did. I don't have to act old anymore; I can simply act my age. Although in the latest movie I've made I did play a man a decade younger. The reality is that I am here and I feel fortunate to be able to be this age. It didn't happen in a day or two, although at times it does seem that time did move that quickly.

But if there is anything that has surprised me about reaching this age with almost full command of my physical and mental capabilities it is how much I still care about those things that have long been important to me and, even more, the fact that I probably am better at some of them than I have ever been. I know I am better at being a husband and a grandfather than I have been. I know my riding ability has continued to improve. And to my surprise, I know without doubt that I am a better actor than I have ever been. The greater control over my instrument, combined with many decades of experience, has enabled me to become a far more complete performer in whatever it is I am doing.

That and the fact that I still care so much about giving the audience its money's worth. I never watch my own performances; it makes me too uncomfortable. And I almost never read reviews. It amazes me that criticism still bothers me. I mean, what damage can criticism do to my career? And yet as an entertainer I still so much want to feel loved by the audience that it bothers me terribly when I'm not, so I'd rather not know.

But I do know who I am. It has taken me a long time to be completely comfortable being Bill Shatner, to get beyond the sometimes protective bravado and accept the fact that it is no longer necessary for me to send myself valentines. I was asked at one point how people react when I walk into a room.

I had to give that some real thought: Mostly, what I feel is their smiles of acknowledgment. I see recognition on their faces and, as a function of age and perhaps accomplishment, respect. It is always, "Mr. Shatner, so nice to meet you. I'm honored." To which I respond, "What are you honored about?" It happens often enough to remind me that I have been around long enough and done enough so that I have become a familiar face. People do think they know me, and depending on their age they know me in different personalities. The oldest people know me as Captain Kirk. People in middle age know me as T. J. Hooker. Younger people know me as Denny Crane. And the youngest people who do know me now recognize me as the Priceline Negotiator.

I am not in any hurry to find out what death is like. The optimist in me finds those positive aspects. Perhaps I won't be lonely anymore. And I doubt I will worry about being broke ever again. And I won't feel the pain of watching a person or an animal I care about suffer. Those aches I feel when I wake up in the morning will finally be gone. But . . . but . . .

I can make the jokes about it: Finally I'll be on time for a funeral! But I will continue to put off that event as long as humanly possible. I have, as Spock wished us all so many years ago, lived long and prospered. And it remains my goal to go where no man has ever gone before. When the time comes, though, I will be so thankful for the good fortune I have been given, for the people who have made this journey with me, for the joy I've found in animals and nature, and then I will fight for one more day. I will, I know I will, do as Dylan Thomas urged and rage, rage against the dying of the light.

ACKNOWLEDGMENTS

I also would like to acknowledge my friend and fellow Yankee fan, the late Carmen La Via. Carmen truly had a lust for life and his many, many friends will hear his laughter echoing in our minds forever. And of course I would like to thank Carmen's longtime associate Peter Sawyer, for his substantial contributions under difficult circumstances. I also want to express my appreciation to Kathleen Hays, who does everything that needs to be done, solves every problem, answers every question, and does so with grace and a smile. She takes the bumps out of the road. Our publisher, Tom Dunne, is simply one of the best people, not just in our business, but on our planet. He cares about the right things and understands the power of the printed word to make a difference. Stephen Power has the great editor's gift of being able to push and pull without leaving his prints on the page; it requires a brightness of personality, knowledge, and taste that I greatly appreciate.

This is a book about aging and in my own life no one does it better than my friend Rich Soll. His never-waning fascination with the eddies of life have long amazed me, and this is my opportunity to tell him how much I appreciate his friendship and his wisdom.

This is the third book I've done with William Shatner. I was an admirer long before we worked together and the projects we've done have only added to that. Here's the fact: Bill Shatner in private is a wonderful, really smart, remarkably creative, and very decent human being. His mind is always reaching someplace new and more often than is generally known it involves finding a way to use his success to help other people. I want him to know how much I enjoy working with him and how deeply I admire him.

And finally, my appreciation to my wife, Laura. I always end acknowledgments by expressing my appreciation to her, but while she is last on the page she always is first in my life. I am a lucky man to have won her heart. She brings joy to every day of my life.
— David Fisher

ABOUT THE AUTHORS

William Shatner has worked as a musician, producer, director, and celebrity pitchman, and notably played Captain Kirk on *Star Trek* from 1966 to 1969 and in seven Star Trek films. He won an Emmy and a Golden Globe for his role as attorney Denny Crane on the TV drama *Boston Legal.* He lives in Los Angeles with his wife, Elizabeth.

David Fisher is the author of more than twenty New York Times bestsellers, including William Shatner's autobiography *Up Till Now* and *Leonard.* He lives in New York.

The employees of Thorndike Press hope you have enjoyed this Large Print book. All our Thorndike, Wheeler, and Kennebec Large Print titles are designed for easy reading, and all our books are made to last. Other Thorndike Press Large Print books are available at your library, through selected bookstores, or directly from us.

For information about titles, please call:
  (800) 223-1244

or visit our website at:
  gale.com/thorndike

To share your comments, please write:
  Publisher
  Thorndike Press
  10 Water St., Suite 310
  Waterville, ME 04901